United States Government Accountability Office
Washington, DC 20548

July 8, 2009

The Honorable Max Baucus
Committee on Finance, Chairman
United States Senate

Subject: *Climate Change Trade Measures: Considerations for U.S. Policy Makers*

Dear Mr. Chairman:

Changes in the earth's climate attributable to increased concentrations of greenhouse gases may have significant environmental and economic impacts in the United States and internationally. To mitigate climate change effects, countries are taking or considering varying approaches to reducing greenhouse gas emissions, such as carbon dioxide, which is the most important greenhouse gas due to its significant volume. These approaches range from measures to increase energy efficiency to longer-term efforts to develop technologies to establish a less carbon-intensive energy infrastructure. A U.S. policy to mitigate climate change may require domestic production facilities to achieve specified reductions or employ a market-based mechanism, such as establishing a price on emissions.

Between 2007 and 2009, Congress introduced a number of climate change bills, many of which contained proposals for a domestic emissions pricing system, such as a cap-and-trade system[1] or a carbon tax[2]. Through greenhouse gas emissions pricing, governments create an incentive for parties to lower their greenhouse gas emissions by placing a cost on them. However, imposing costs on energy-intensive industries in the United States could potentially place them at a disadvantage to foreign competitors. In addition, emissions pricing could have negative environmental consequences, such as "carbon leakage," whereby emissions reductions in the United States are replaced by increases in production and emissions in less-regulated countries. As the Congress considers the design of a domestic emissions pricing system, a key challenge will be balancing the need to reduce greenhouse gas emissions with the need to address the competitiveness of U.S. industries.

In anticipation of Senate deliberation on climate change legislative proposals, you asked us to examine how greenhouse gas emissions pricing could potentially affect the international competitiveness of U.S. industries, and to examine trade measures being considered as part

---

[1] A cap-and-trade system is an emissions pricing system in which the government applies an aggregate cap or quota to limit total emissions from regulated sources, which are required to hold allowances to cover their emissions. Allowances are allocated by the government and may be traded. Sources whose allowances exceed their emissions may offer permits for sale, while sources for which emissions exceed allowances will need to buy them.

[2] Under a carbon tax system, regulated sources pay a charge based on the level of their emissions.

of proposed U.S. climate change legislation.[3] On July 6, 2009, we briefed your staff covering: (1) what is known about estimating industry effects, (2) examples of industries that may be vulnerable to a loss in international competitiveness from emissions pricing, (3) trade measures and other approaches to address competitiveness issues, and (4) the potential international implications of trade measures. A copy of the slides presented at the briefing is attached.

To address these objectives, we interviewed officials and reviewed climate change literature and documents from relevant federal agencies, international organizations, policy institutes, businesses, professional organizations, and universities; reviewed and analyzed climate change legislation introduced between 2007 and 2009 and congressional hearing records; we reviewed and presented summary results for two studies that attempt to quantify the potential international competitiveness effects on domestic industries from greenhouse gas emissions pricing; and conducted interviews with officials from the embassies of Australia, Brazil, Canada, China, the European Union, and Mexico. We conducted our work from October 2008 to July 2009 in accordance with all sections of GAO's Quality Assurance Framework that are relevant to our objectives. The framework requires that we plan and perform the engagement to obtain sufficient and appropriate evidence to meet our stated objectives and to discuss any limitations in our work. We believe that the information and data obtained, and the analysis conducted, provide a reasonable basis for any findings and conclusions in this product. For additional details regarding our scope and methodology, see appendix I.

We are sending copies of this report to interested congressional committees and to other parties. In addition, the report will be available at no charge on GAO's Web site at http://www.gao.gov.

If you or your staff have any questions or wish to discuss this material further, please contact me at (202) 512-4347 or yagerl@gao.gov. Contact points for our Offices of Congressional Relations and Public Affairs may be found on the last page of this report. Christine Broderick (Assistant Director), Etana Finkler, Kendall Helm, Jeremy Latimer, Maria Mercado, and Ardith Spence, made significant contributions to this report. In addition, Karen Deans, David Dornisch, Grace Lui, and Jena Sinkfield provided technical assistance.

Sincerely yours,

Loren Yager
Director, International Affairs and Trade

---

[3]You also asked GAO to examine revenue measures under consideration as part of climate change legislation. GAO plans to issue this product later in 2009.

CLIMATE CHANGE TRADE MEASURES

Considerations for U.S. Policy Makers

Why GAO Did This Study

Global climate change is one of the most significant long-term policy challenges facing the United States, and policies to mitigate climate change will have important economic, social, and environmental implications.

Members of Congress have introduced several bills to address the problem of climate change, many of which establish domestic emissions pricing by requiring firms that emit greenhouse gases either to pay a tax or to hold emission allowances. Whichever approach is taken, domestic emissions pricing could produce environmental benefits by encouraging U.S. firms to reduce their emissions of greenhouse gases. But such pricing could also harm U.S. firms' competitiveness, especially in energy-intensive industries where firms compete internationally. Additionally, there could be increased emissions abroad if production were to increase in other countries as a result of increased domestic costs of production resulting from a U.S. climate policy (carbon leakage). To help reduce impacts on U.S. firms and prevent carbon leakage, several climate change bills have also included trade measures or output-based rebates. The bills have included trade measures that would require importers to purchase emission allowances or pay a border tax for the greenhouse gas emissions associated with their imports. They have also designed output-based rebates to financially rebate industries for the costs incurred under a domestic emissions pricing system.

Briefing Structure

Estimating Industry Effects: Estimating the potential effects of domestic emissions pricing for industries in the United States is complex. If the United States were to regulate greenhouse gas emissions, production costs could rise for certain industries and could cause output, profits, or employment to fall. Within these industries, some of these adverse effects could arise through an increase in imports, a decrease in exports, or both. Estimates of adverse competitiveness effects are generally larger for industries that are both relatively energy and trade intensive. In 2007, these industries accounted for about 4.5 percent of domestic output.

Estimates of the effects vary because of key assumptions required by economic models. For example, models generally assume a price for U.S. carbon emissions, but do not assume a similar price by other nations. In addition, the models generally do not incorporate all policy provisions, such as legislative proposals related to trade measures and rebates that are based on levels of production.

Potentially Vulnerable Industries: Proposed legislation suggests that industries vulnerable to competitiveness effects should be considered differently. Industries for which competitiveness measures would apply are identified on the basis of their energy and trade intensity. Most of the industries that meet these criteria are in primary metals, nonmetallic minerals, paper, and chemicals, although significant variation exists for product groups (sub-industries) within each industry. Additional variation arises on the basis of the type of energy used and the extent to which foreign competitors' greenhouse gas emissions are regulated.

To illustrate variability in characteristics that make industries vulnerable to competitiveness effects, we selected example sub-industries within primary metals, non metallic minerals, paper products, and chemicals based on multiple factors. For example, we selected sub-industries that met both the energy and trade intensity criteria, examples that met only one criterion, and examples that met neither, but had significant imports from countries without greenhouse-gas pricing.

Trade Measures: Trade measures have been proposed to help address potential industry and environmental effects of a domestic emissions pricing system; however, questions exist about their proposed effectiveness. Supporters argue that trade measures may help prevent a decline in output by U.S. producers, prevent carbon leakage, and create leverage for other

Objectives, Scope, and Methodology

GAO was asked to examine the potential effects of greenhouse gas emissions pricing on U.S. industries' international competitiveness and trade measures being considered as part of U.S. legislative proposals to address climate change.

Specifically, we examined: (1) what is known about estimating industry effects; (2) examples of industries that may be vulnerable to a loss in international competitiveness from emissions pricing; (3) trade measures and other approaches to address competitiveness issues; and (4) potential international implications of trade measures.

To address these objectives, we interviewed officials and reviewed climate change literature and documents from U.S. agencies, international organizations, policy institutes, and professional organizations; reviewed and analyzed climate change legislation introduced between 2007 and 2009 and congressional hearing records; reviewed and presented summary results for two studies attempting to quantify the potential international competitiveness effects on domestic industries from emissions pricing; and conducted interviews with officials from the embassies of Australia, Brazil, Canada, China, the European Union, and Mexico.

The Office of the United States Trade Representative provided technical comments on this report.

The analysis in this report reflects changes to the American Clean Energy and Security Act of 2009 (HR 2454), as of June 26, 2009.

For additional details regarding our scope and methodology, see appendix I.

countries to reduce emissions. Opponents raise concerns that trade measures may motivate retaliatory actions, undermine efforts to secure multilateral consensus, and generate little leverage. In addition, potential implementation challenges may exist.

Output-based rebates are measures that offset incurred costs to industries due to emissions pricing and can take the form of a per-unit rebate, allocation of allowances or tax credit. These rebates have been proposed to address competitiveness effects; however, limitations with these measures may also exist. For example, output-based rebates may increase costs for industries that do not receive them, under certain conditions.

How a trade measure is ultimately designed will have important implications for the effectiveness of the overall measure in addressing industry and environmental effects. For example, delaying the timing for when the trade measure goes into effect could result in the measure being a more effective leveraging tool, and would provide other countries an opportunity to implement similar carbon mitigation policies to reduce global emissions. On the other hand, having the trade measure go into effect simultaneously when the domestic cap-and-trade system goes into effect may reduce impacts on U.S. industry competitiveness.

International Trade Implications: A unilateral U.S. trade measure could have important international implications on U.S. bilateral and multilateral trade relations. For example, other countries could view U.S. trade measures as trade restrictions or sanctions, which could lead them to implement restrictions against U.S. exports. Attention also has focused on the potential for trade measures or output-based rebates to be challenged under World Trade Organization (WTO) rules.

Assessing the international trade implications is difficult for a number of reasons. One is that it depends in part upon how other nations reduce their carbon emissions, and whether they perceive any U.S. measures as likely to affect their exports. In addition, the outcome of any WTO challenge, if any, would be uncertain and may depend on how the measure is implemented.

Background

GREENHOUSE GAS EMISSIONS

The Greenhouse Effect

Greenhouse gases, such as carbon dioxide, methane, nitrous oxide, and other gases, increase temperatures by trapping heat that would otherwise escape the earth's atmosphere. The heat-trapping effect, known as the greenhouse effect, moderates atmospheric temperatures, keeping the earth warm enough to support life. Although each unit of non-carbon-dioxide greenhouse gas generally has a greater warming effect than each unit of carbon dioxide, carbon dioxide is the most important greenhouse gas because of its significant volume. The potency of other greenhouse gases may be expressed in terms of their warming potential relative to carbon dioxide, or their carbon dioxide equivalent.

Estimated Growth in Emissions

According to the IPCC, in 2004, developed countries, including the United States, constituted 20 percent of the global population, but were responsible for nearly half of global greenhouse gas emissions. However, the IPCC projects that between 2000 and 2030, two-thirds to three-quarters of the projected increase in global carbon dioxide emissions will occur in developing countries. The IPCC also projects that compared with 2000, global greenhouse gas emissions will increase between 25 percent and 90 percent by 2030 in the absence of policies to reduce greenhouse gas emissions worldwide.

The Intergovernmental Panel on Climate Change (IPCC) was established to provide scientific and objective information on climate change. According to the IPCC, global atmospheric concentrations of greenhouse gases have increased markedly as a result of human activities over the past 200 years, contributing to a warming of the earth's climate. Climate change is a long-term and global issue because greenhouse gases disperse widely in the atmosphere once emitted and can remain there for an extended period of time. Among other potential impacts, climate change could threaten coastal areas with rising sea levels, alter agricultural productivity, and increase the intensity and frequency of floods and tropical storms. While the effect of increases in greenhouse gas emissions on ecosystems and economic growth is expected to vary across regions, countries, and economic sectors, a panel of 18 climate change economists convened by GAO in coordination with the National Academy of Sciences agreed that the Congress should consider using a market-based mechanism to place a price on emissions, and 14 of the 18 panelists were at least moderately confident that the benefits of taking these actions would outweigh the costs. See GAO-08-605.

As shown in figure 1, the United States emitted more carbon dioxide than any other country in 2006, while China recently surpassed the European countries that are members of the Organization for Economic Cooperation and Development (OECD) as the world's second largest emitter. On a per capita basis, the United States and Canada rank first and second in carbon dioxide emissions. Between 1990 and 2006, carbon dioxide emissions grew substantially in both China and India.

Figure 1: Data on Global Carbon Dioxide Emissions

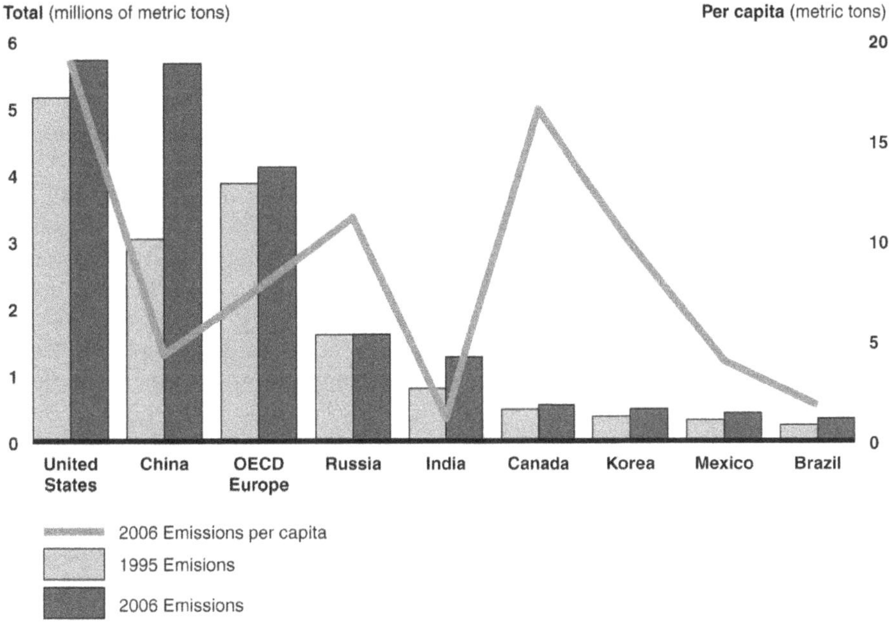

Source: International Energy Agency data on carbon dioxide emissions from fuel consumption.

Background

INTERNATIONAL NEGOTIATIONS AND EMISSIONS PRICING

The Kyoto Protocol

The Kyoto Protocol, adopted in Kyoto, Japan, and ratified by more than 180 countries, sets legally binding emissions targets for 37 industrialized countries and the European Community (Annex I countries).

The Bali Action Plan

The year 2012 will mark the end of the first commitment period of the Kyoto Protocol. In Bali, Indonesia, in 2007, countries agreed to the Bali Action Plan, which defined a process and timeframe to enable the full effective and sustained implementation of the Convention through long-term cooperative action up to and beyond 2012. According to the Bali Action Plan, the negotiations process is scheduled to conclude in December 2009 at a major summit in Copenhagen, Denmark.

Existing Emissions Pricing Systems

Greenhouse gas emissions pricing has been implemented in several other cases, including a cap-and-trade system in the European Union (EU) and carbon tax systems in Sweden, Finland, Norway, and the Netherlands. The world's largest emissions pricing system, the European Union Emissions Trading Scheme (EU ETS), covers CO_2 emissions from more than 11,000 energy-intensive installations. The EU ETS began with a pilot phase that ran from 2005 to 2007. Its second trading period is currently under way. For more information see GAO-09-151.

Greenhouse gas emissions reductions in all major countries will be required to stabilize greenhouse gas concentrations at a level that would prevent dangerous climate change. In 1992, 192 countries, including the United States, joined the United Nations Framework Convention on Climate Change (UNFCCC), an international treaty to consider what may be done to reduce and adapt to global warming. In 1998, the United States signed the Kyoto Protocol, an international agreement to specifically limit greenhouse gas emissions. The United States is not bound by the protocol's terms because it was not ratified by the Senate. Both the UNFCCC and the Kyoto protocol operate under the principal of "common but differentiated responsibilities" to reflect the agreement that each nation must contribute to addressing climate change, but that the magnitude of its efforts should differ according to national circumstances. For example, under the protocol, only Annex I countries have quantified emission reduction obligations. To negotiate the next round of international commitments, parties to the UNFCCC agreed to the "Bali Action Plan" in December 2007.

Countries can take varying approaches to reducing greenhouse gas emissions. Since energy use is a significant source of greenhouse gas emissions, policies designed to increase energy efficiency or induce a switch to less greenhouse gas-intensive fuels, such as from coal to natural gas, can reduce emissions in the short term. In the long term, however, major technology changes will be needed to establish a less carbon-intensive energy infrastructure. To that end, a U.S. policy to mitigate climate change may require facilities to achieve specified reductions or employ a market-based mechanism, such as establishing a price on emissions.

Proposed Legislation Includes Two Options for Domestic Emissions Pricing Systems

Through greenhouse gas emissions pricing, governments create an incentive for parties to lower their greenhouse gas emissions by placing a cost on the emissions. Proposed U.S. legislation includes two basic approaches to greenhouse gas emissions pricing: a carbon tax system and a cap-and-trade system. A carbon tax system would impose a fee on emissions of greenhouse gases. Under a cap-and-trade system, the government would cap greenhouse gas emissions, limiting the total quantity of emissions from regulated sources under the system. The government would also issue allowances, or permits to emit greenhouse gases, equal to the overall cap or quota. Regulated sources would be required to hold enough allowances to cover their emissions, and allowances could be bought and sold as needed to meet the system's requirements in the least expensive manner.

Several bills to implement emissions pricing in the United States have been introduced in the 110th and the 111th Congresses. These bills have included both cap-and-trade and carbon tax proposals. Some of the proposed legislation also include measures intended to limit potentially adverse impacts on the international competitiveness of domestic firms.

Estimating Industry Effects

1

INTRODUCTION:

In this section, we present information on what is known about how U.S. emissions pricing could potentially affect industry competitiveness. Importantly, estimating the effects of domestic emissions pricing for industries in the United States is complex. For example, if the United States were to regulate greenhouse gas emissions, production costs could rise for many industries and could cause output, profits, or employment to fall. However, the magnitude of these potential effects is likely to depend on the greenhouse gas intensity of industry output and on the domestic emissions price, which is not yet known, among other factors. Additionally, if U.S. climate policy were more stringent than in other countries, some domestic industries could experience a loss in international competitiveness. Within these industries, adverse competitiveness effects could arise through an increase in imports, a decrease in exports, or both.

To estimate the potential economic effects of U.S. emissions pricing on domestic industries, models require key assumptions, which cause estimates to vary. In this section, we review two economic models that specifically estimate competitiveness effects for U.S. industries. In each, larger adverse effects occur for those U.S. industries that are both relatively energy and trade intensive. We also present information on the potential for adverse international competitiveness effects to be a source of carbon leakage.

U.S. emissions pricing effects on production costs and output

For regulated sources, greenhouse gas emissions pricing would increase the cost of releasing greenhouse gases. As a result, it would encourage some of these sources to reduce their emissions, compared with business-as-usual. Under domestic emissions pricing, production costs for regulated sources could rise as they either take action to reduce their emissions or pay for the greenhouse gases they release. Cost increases are likely to be larger for production that is relatively greenhouse gas intensive, where greenhouse gas intensity refers to emissions per unit of output. Cost increases may reduce industry profits, or they may be passed on to consumers in the form of higher prices. To the extent that cost increases are passed on to consumers, they could demand fewer goods, and industry output could fall.

While emissions pricing would likely cause production costs to rise for certain industries, the extent of this rise and the resulting impact on industry output are less certain due to a number of factors. For example, the U.S. emissions price and the emissions price in other countries are key variables that will help to determine the impact of emissions pricing on domestic industries. However, future emission prices are currently unknown. Furthermore, to the extent that emissions pricing encourages technological change that reduces greenhouse gas intensity, potential adverse effects of emissions pricing on profits or output could be mitigated for U.S. industries. Additionally, policy options such as output-based rebates could also offset some of the added costs of emissions pricing for some firms but involve tradeoffs, such as possibly increasing costs for firms that do not receive them.

Estimating Industry Effects

1

Estimated effects from economic models of emissions pricing

Several studies by U.S. agencies and experts have used models of the economy to simulate the effects of emissions pricing policy on output and related economic outcomes. These models generally find that emissions pricing will cause output, profits or employment to decline in sectors that are described as energy intensive, compared with business-as-usual. In general, these studies conclude that these declines are likely to be greater for these industries, as compared to other sectors in the economy. However, some research suggests that not every industry is likely to suffer adverse effects from emissions pricing. For example, a long-run model estimated by Ho, Morgenstern, and Shih (2008) predicts that some U.S. sectors, such as services, may experience growth in the long run as a result of domestic emissions pricing. This growth would likely be due to changes in consumption patterns in favor of goods and services that are relatively less greenhouse gas intensive.

Potential international competitiveness effects depend in part on the stringency of U.S. climate policy relative to other countries. For example, if domestic greenhouse gas emissions pricing were to make emissions more expensive in the United States than in other countries, production costs for domestic industries would likely increase relative to their international competitors, potentially disadvantaging industries in the United States. As a result, some domestic production could shift abroad, through changes in consumption or investment patterns, to countries where greenhouse gas emissions are less stringently regulated. For example, consumers may substitute some goods made in other countries for some goods made domestically. Similarly, investment patterns could shift more strongly in favor of new capacity in countries where greenhouse gas emissions are regulated less stringently than in the United States.

Economists such as Aldy and Pizer (2009) have defined adverse international competitiveness effects as the part of a decline in domestic output that is due to a shift of production abroad in response to emissions pricing, or the part of a decline in domestic output that not also matched by a decline in domestic consumption. For example, if domestic output were to fall by more than domestic consumption, the difference could be explained by changes in trade patterns through a reduction in exports, an increase in imports, or both.

Estimating Industry Effects

Factors that may affect international competitiveness

Stakeholders and experts have identified two criteria, among others, that are important in determining potential vulnerability to adverse competitiveness effects: trade intensity and energy intensity. Trade intensity is important because international competitiveness effects arise from changes in trade patterns. For example, if climate policy in the United States were more stringent than in other countries, international competition could limit the ability of domestic firms to pass increases in costs through to consumers. Energy intensity is important because the combustion of fossil fuels for energy is a significant source of greenhouse gas emissions, which may increase production costs under emissions pricing. International competitiveness effects may also depend on other factors, including transportation costs and access to markets for natural resources, capital, or labor.

Industries that are both relatively trade intensive and energy intensive include primary metals, nonmetallic minerals, paper products, and chemicals. These four industries provided around 4.5 percent of total U.S. output in 2007.

Legislation passed in June 2009 by the House of Representatives, H.R. 2454, 111th Cong. (2009), uses the criteria of trade intensity and energy intensity or greenhouse gas intensity, among others, to determine eligibility for the Emission Allowance Rebate Program that is part of the legislation. H.R. 2454 specifies how to calculate the two criteria. Trade intensity is defined as the ratio of the sum of the value of imports and exports within an industry to the sum of the value of shipments (output) and imports within the industry. Energy intensity is defined as the industry's cost of purchased electricity and fuel costs, or energy expenditures, divided by the value of shipments (output) of the industry.

The energy intensity measure specified in this legislation, however, might not be an ideal measure of vulnerability. First, the relationship between energy expenditures and emissions from energy use is indeterminate. For example, energy expenditures depend on the price of fuel and on the quantity of fuel used, while emissions from energy use depend on the quantity and type of fuel used. Additionally, an increase in energy prices may cause expenditures on energy to rise and energy use to fall, which could also cause emissions from energy use to fall. Second, the energy intensity measure might not reflect the extent to which substitutes for energy are available. For example, regulated sources may be able to reduce their energy intensity or switch to energy sources that are less greenhouse gas intensive. To the extent that less greenhouse gas intensive substitutes are available, some industries could reduce the effect of emissions pricing on their costs and on their competitiveness.

Estimating Industry Effects

1

Key assumptions of models that estimate competitiveness effects

Key assumptions made by economic models of emissions pricing include, among others, the domestic emissions price, the emissions price in other countries, the level of industry aggregation, and the time horizon during which producers may adjust their production methods or energy sources in response to emissions pricing.

- *Domestic emissions price:* The domestic emissions price could affect the size of a potential increase in production costs from emissions pricing. In particular, increases in production costs are expected to be larger when the domestic emissions price is greater. Under a carbon tax system, the domestic emissions price would equal the tax per unit of emissions. Under a cap-and-trade system, the domestic emissions price would equal the market-clearing allowance price, at which the quantity of allowances supplied equals the quantity of allowances demanded.

   The domestic emissions price could also depend on cost containment features of an emissions pricing system, such as banking, borrowing or carbon offsets, among other features.

- *Emissions price in other countries:* Together with the domestic emissions price, the emissions price in other countries will help to determine the relative stringency of climate policy in the United States. When the difference between the domestic emissions price and a lower emissions price in other countries is larger, U.S. industries may be more likely to experience adverse competitiveness effects from domestic emissions pricing. Under a cap-and-trade system, differences in the allowance price between two countries may dissipate if international trading of allowances is allowed.

- *Level of aggregation:* The range of estimated effects may depend on the level of industrial or sectoral aggregation used. For example, estimates for highly aggregated sectors could mask more extreme variation at the more narrowly aggregated sub-industry level.

- *Time horizon:* In models of economic activity, the amount of time considered after policy implementation may affect model results. For example, the time horizon may affect the ability of firms to pass through added costs to consumers in the form of higher prices, change their production processes, or develop and adopt new technologies. A longer time horizon could also allow for investments in new capacity.

- *Policy Scenarios:* Model results may depend in part upon the range of policy scenarios incorporated. For example the incorporation of trade measures and output-based rebates may affect the results.

1

Estimates of competitiveness effects are uncertain

Table 1 presents results from two studies that attempt to quantify the potential competitiveness effects on domestic industries from emissions pricing. For each study, a range of estimates is reported for two effects: (1) the potential decline in domestic, energy-intensive manufacturing output that is due to U.S. emissions pricing and (2) the part of this decline that is due to adverse international competitiveness effects. The adverse competitiveness effects are computed as the difference between the production and consumption impacts of emissions pricing. For example, if production declines by 3.7 percent and consumption declines by 2.9 percent as a share of production, the adverse competitiveness effect equals the -0.8 percent change in production that is not matched by a change in domestic consumption.

In both studies, estimates of competitiveness effects are generally greater for industries that are relatively trade and energy intensive.

The estimated impacts depend on key assumptions of the models used to generate these results. Both studies assume unilateral action by the United States, or an emissions price of $0 per ton of carbon dioxide in the rest of the world, which may overstate the estimates of adverse competitiveness effects for U.S. industries to the extent that other countries also regulate greenhouse gas emissions.

Aldy and Pizer's (2009) model allows for some adjustments and is consistent with a time horizon of 1 year to a few years. Ho et al. (2008) generate their long-run estimates using a model that allows for more adjustments.

Table 1: Estimates of Emissions Pricing Effects on Energy-Intensive Manufacturing Industries in the United States

	Study	
	Aldy and Pizer (2009)	**Ho, Morgenstern, and Shih (2008)**
Estimated decline in industry output due to emissions pricing (range of estimates)	1.0% – 4.3%	0.91% - 1.30%
Part of estimated decline in industry output due to adverse international competitiveness effects (range of estimates)	0.3% – 1.8%	0.42% - 0.68%
Domestic emissions price (per ton of carbon dioxide)	$15	$10
Emissions price in other countries (per ton of carbon dioxide)	$0	$0
Time horizon	1 year to a few years	Long run
Number of industries in model	400+	21
Number of industries for which results are reported by authors	55 energy-intensive	21
Number of industries included in the ranges of estimates reported above	55	3 most energy-intensive
Incorporation of trade measure and output-based rebate policies	no	no

Source: GAO analysis of results reported by Aldy and Pizer (2009) and Ho, Morgenstern, and Shih (2008). Note: The number of industries in both reflects, in part, the level of industry aggregation. While Aldy and Pizer (2009) examine more than 400 industries at a more narrowly aggregated level, they report estimates only for 55 energy-intensive industries among the more than 400 industries they examine. Ho et al. (2008) examine industries at a more aggregated level and report estimates for all 21 manufacturing and nonmanufacturing sectors that they consider. Ho et al. (2008) also report estimates of the effects of emissions pricing on industry output for multiple time horizons, but they report both production and consumption effects—both of which are necessary to compute competitiveness effects—only for their long run estimates. For the study by Aldy and Pizer (2009), the estimated decline in industry output and the part that is due to competitiveness effects are reported as a percentage of industry output. For the study by Ho et al. (2008), the estimated decline in industry output and the part that is due to competitiveness effects are reported as a share of sectoral consumption.

1

International competitiveness effects and carbon leakage

Reducing carbon emissions in the United States could result in carbon leakage through two potential mechanisms. First, if domestic production were to shift abroad to countries where greenhouse gas emissions are not regulated, emissions in these countries could grow faster than expected otherwise. Through this mechanism, some of the expected benefits of reducing emissions domestically could be offset by faster growth in emissions elsewhere, according to Aldy and Pizer (2009).

Carbon leakage may also arise from changes in world prices that are brought about by domestic emissions pricing. For example, U.S. emissions pricing could cause domestic demand for oil to fall. Because the United States is a relatively large consumer of oil worldwide, the world price of oil could fall when the U.S. demand for oil drops. The quantity of oil consumed by other countries would rise in response, increasing greenhouse gas emissions from the rest of the world. These price effects may be a more important source of carbon leakage than the trade effects described above. See Fischer and Fox (2009) and EPA (2009).

2

INTRODUCTION:

Energy and trade intensities of the four manufacturing industries, in the aggregate, generally meet both vulnerability criteria in proposed legislation. As shown along the right axis in figure 2, nonmetallic minerals is the most energy intensive at 6.1 percent in 2006. As shown along the left axis, chemicals is the most trade intensive, at 45 percent in 2007. While chemicals does not have an energy intensity of 5 percent or greater — and is located outside of the shaded area— several sub-industries within chemicals meet that vulnerability criterion.

Together, these four industries provided 23 percent of total U.S. manufacturing output in 2007 and had trade flows of about $500 billion. As shown by the size of the column, chemicals is the largest industry, with output of $664 billion in 2007. Accordingly, chemicals also accounted for the largest share of carbon dioxide emissions from manufacturing, at 22 percent in 2002. However, the estimated greenhouse gas intensity of chemical products— the level of carbon dioxide emitted per unit of energy—was less than that for both primary metals and nonmetallic minerals in 2002.

In this section, we provide some information on certain U.S. industries that, by paying a price on greenhouse gas emissions, could potentially lose competitiveness compared with foreign industries without comparable climate policies. Among many factors, two key indicators of potential vulnerability to adverse competitiveness effects are an industry's energy intensity and trade intensity. Proposed U.S. legislation specifies that: (a) either an energy intensity or greenhouse gas intensity of 5 percent or greater; and (b) a trade intensity of 15 percent or greater be used as criteria to identify industries for which trade measures or rebates would apply. Since data on greenhouse gas intensity is less complete, we focus our analysis on industry energy intensity. Most of the industries that meet these criteria are in primary metals, nonmetallic minerals, paper, and chemicals, yet there is significant variation in specified vulnerability characteristics among different product groups ("sub-industries"). The following pages include examples of this variation, as well as information on the type of energy used and location of import and export markets. Data shown are for the latest year available, with additional discussion of proposed vulnerability criteria in appendix I and industry information in appendix II.

Figure 2: Energy and Trade Intensity Are Indicators of Vulnerability

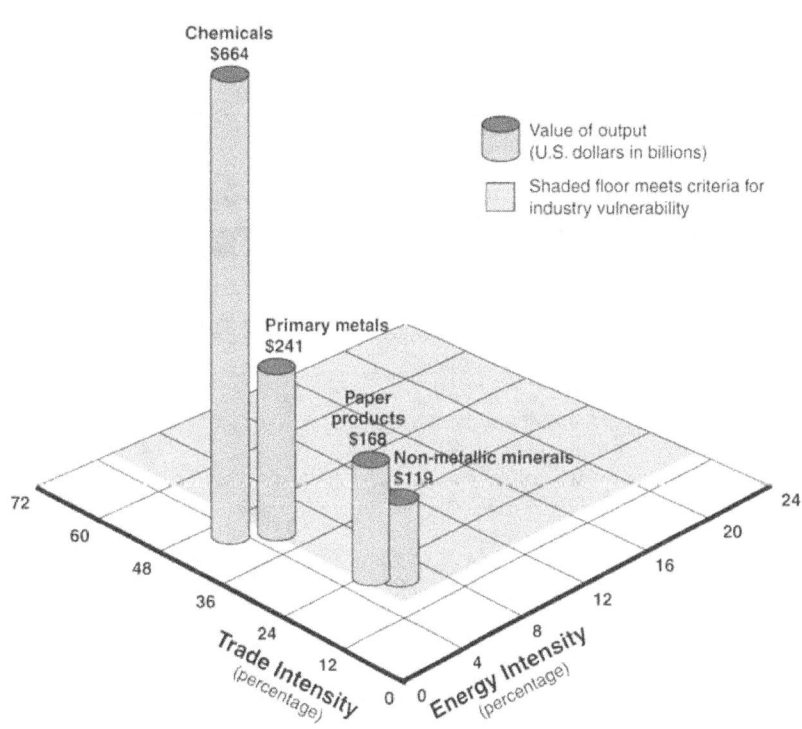

Source: GAO analysis of Department of Energy emissions data and Department of Commerce energy data for 2006 and trade and output data for 2007.

Notes to figure 2

Potentially Vulnerable Industries

PRIMARY METALS EXAMPLES

As shown by sub-industry examples in figure 3, energy and trade intensities differ within primary metals. For example, primary aluminum meets the vulnerability criteria with an energy intensity of 24 percent and trade intensity of 62 percent. Ferrous metal foundries meets the energy intensity criteria, but not the trade intensity criteria. Steel manufacturing—products made from purchased steel—and aluminum products fall short of both vulnerability criteria. Iron and steel mills has an energy intensity of 7 percent and a trade intensity of 35 percent and is by far the largest sub-industry example, with a 2007 value of output of over $93 billion.

Among the primary metals sub-industry examples, types of energy used also vary. Iron and steel mills use the greatest share of coal and coke, and steel manufacturing and ferrous metal foundries use the greatest proportion of natural gas. Since coal is more carbon intensive than natural gas, sub-industries that rely more heavily on coal could also be more vulnerable to competitiveness effects. The carbon intensity of electricity, used heavily in the production of aluminum, will also vary on the basis of source of energy used to generate it and the market conditions where it is sold. Data shown for "aluminum" include primary aluminum and aluminum products and net electricity is the sum of net transfers plus purchases and generation minus quantities sold.

Figure 3: Energy and Trade Intensity Indicators Vary by Sub-Industry

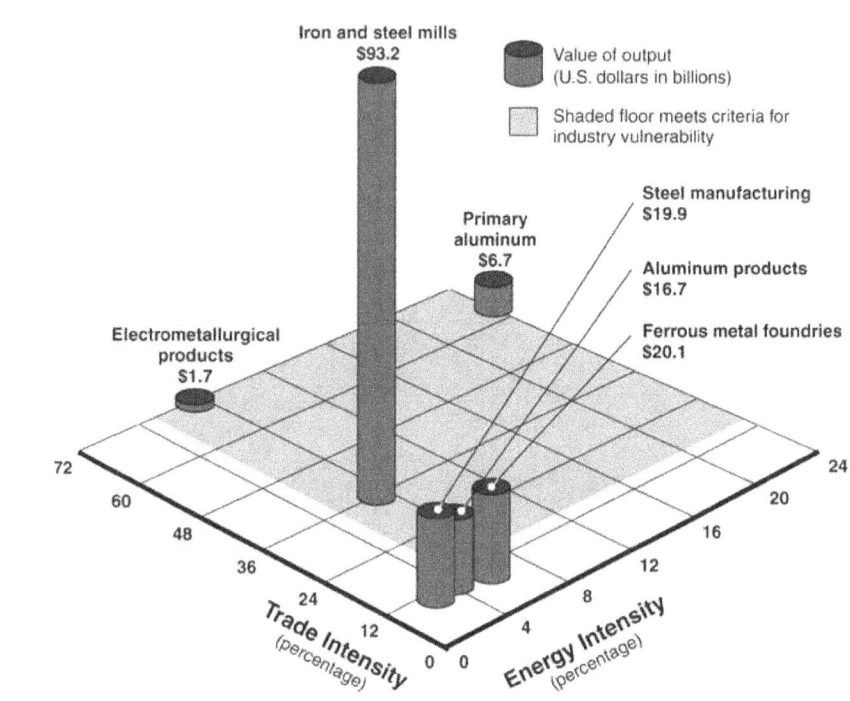

Source: GAO analysis of Department of Commerce energy data for 2006 and trade data for 2007.

Notes to figure 3

Figure 4: Type of Energy Used Is Important for Carbon Intensity

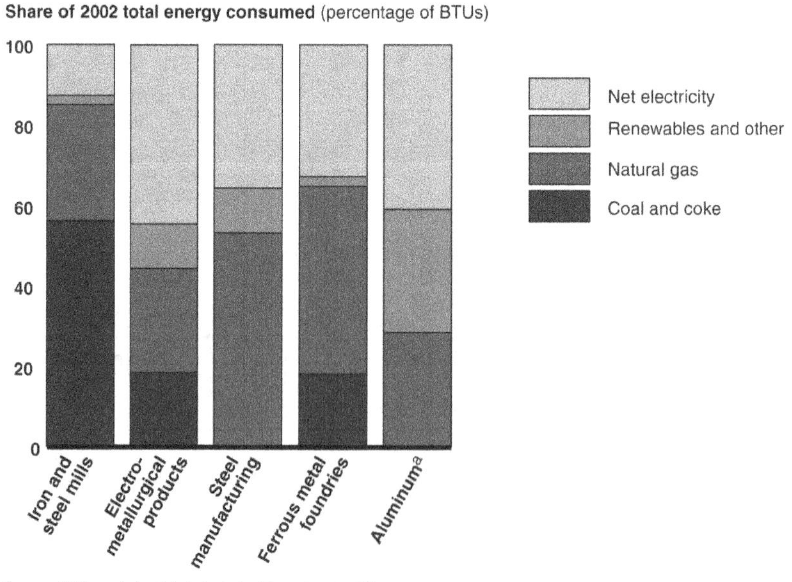

Share of 2002 total energy consumed (percentage of BTUs)

Source: GAO analysis of data from the Department of Energy.

Notes to figure 4

2.1

PRIMARY METALS EXAMPLES

Industry vulnerability may further vary depending on the share of trade with countries that do not have carbon pricing. To illustrate this variability, figure 5 provides data on the share of imports by source, since imports exceed exports in each of the primary metals examples. As shown, while primary aluminum is among the most trade intensive, the majority of imports are from Canada, an Annex I country with agreed emission reduction targets. For iron and steel mills, over one-third of imports are from the EU and other Annex I countries, not including Canada ("EU plus"). However, for iron and steel mills, almost 30 percent of imports are also from the non-Annex I countries of China, Mexico, and Brazil. While less trade intensive, steel manufacturing and aluminum products each has greater than one-third of imports from China alone.

Adverse competitiveness effects from emissions pricing could increase the already growing share of Chinese imports that exists in some of the sub-industries. Among the examples, iron and steel mills, steel manufacturing, and aluminum products exhibit a growing trade reliance on Chinese imports since 2002. This trend has largely been driven by lower labor and capital costs in China and, according to representatives from the steel industry, China has recently been producing 50 percent of the world's steel.

Figure 5: Source of Imports Is Important for Trade Intensity

Share of 2007 total U.S. imports

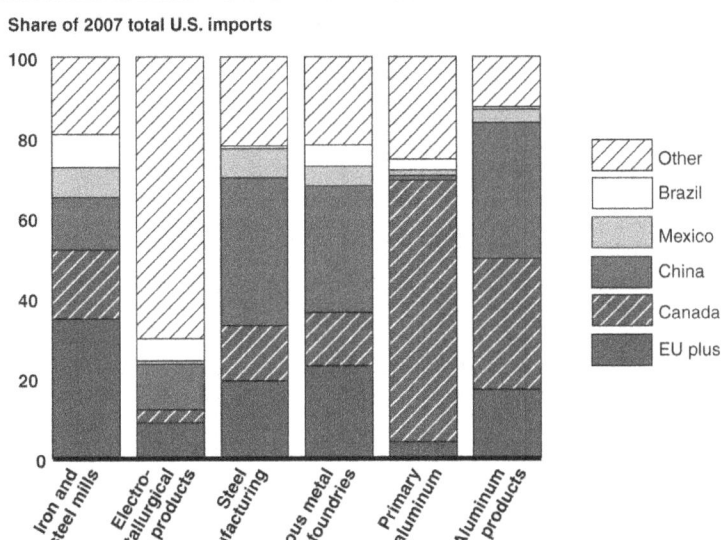

Source: GAO analysis of data from the Department of Commerce.

Notes to figure 5

Figure 6: Sub-Industries With Growing Share of Imports from China

Chinese imports as a share of total U.S. imports (percentage)

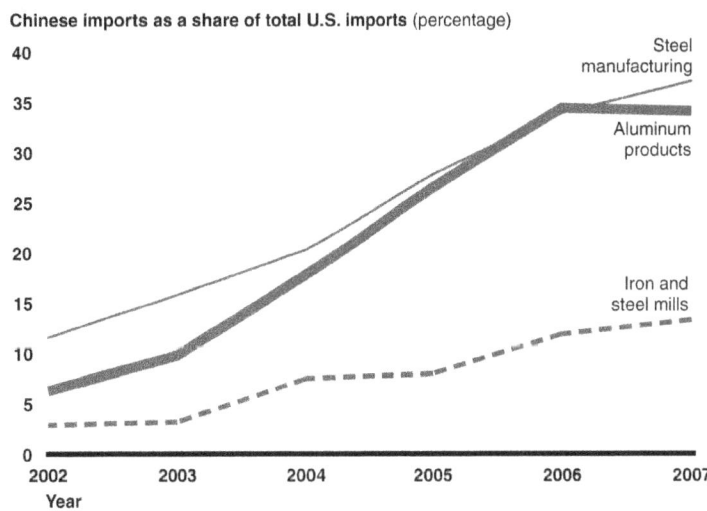

Total U.S. imports by value (U.S. dollars in millions)						
Year	2002	2003	2004	2005	2006	2007
Iron and steel mills	$12,558	10,808	23,355	25,131	33,060	30,445
Steel manufacturing	$1,110	1,184	1,792	1,884	1,916	1,822
Aluminum products	$498	549	718	913	1,209	1,183

Source: GAO analysis of data from the Department of Commerce.

Notes to figure 6

2.2

NONMETALLIC MINERALS EXAMPLES

Among nonmetallic minerals sub-industry examples, cement has the highest energy intensity, at 16 percent, and glass and clay building materials have the highest trade intensity, at 36 percent and 35 percent, respectively. While, concrete is the largest sub-industry, with a value of output of over $30 billion in 2007, it fails to meet both of the vulnerability criteria and thus lies outside of the shaded floor area. Lime and gypsum meets the energy intensity criteria but fails to meet the trade intensity criteria.

Cement and lime rely on coal and coke sources for about 60 percent of energy consumed, while glass and mineral wool rely on natural gas for over 65 percent of energy consumed. Since coal is more carbon intensive than natural gas, sub-industries that rely more heavily on coal could also be more vulnerable to competitiveness effects. Data on energy use by the sub-industry examples excluded from the chart are not currently reported by the Department of Energy.

Figure 7: Energy and Trade Intensity Indicators Vary by Sub-Industry

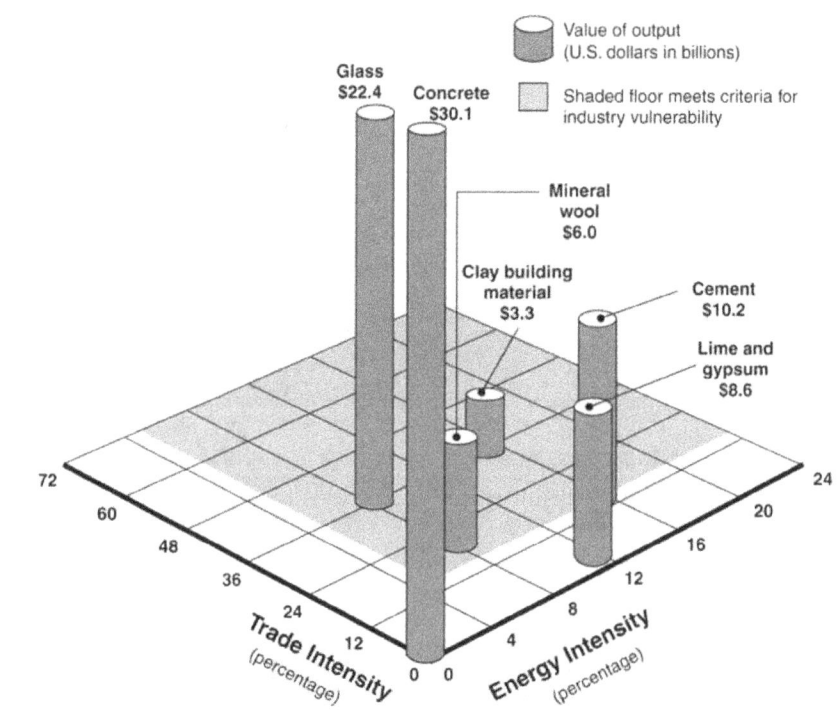

Source: GAO analysis of Department of Commerce energy data for 2006 and trade and output data for 2007.

Notes to figure 7

Figure 8: Type of Energy Used Is Important for Carbon Intensity

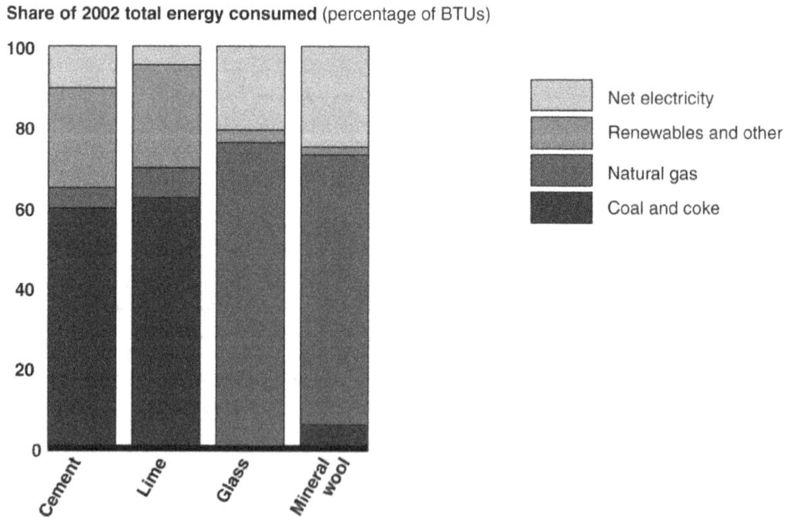

Share of 2002 total energy consumed (percentage of BTUs)

Net electricity
Renewables and other
Natural gas
Coal and coke

Source: GAO analysis of data from the Department of Energy.

Notes to figure 8

2.2

Potentially Vulnerable Industries

NONMETALLIC MINERALS EXAMPLES

For the nonmetallic mineral examples, total imports exceed total exports. As shown in figure 9, glass has the largest share of imports from China, at 26 percent. Another 17 percent of glass imports are sourced from Mexico. For the other trade-intensive sub-industries of cement, clay building material, and mineral wool, about 30 percent of imports are from China, Mexico, and Brazil. Conversely, nearly 60 percent of lime and gypsum imports are from Canada.

The one sub-industry where exports comprise more than 60 percent of trade flows is concrete, with 30 percent of concrete exports sold to markets in Mexico and the Middle East.

Since 2002, a trend of increasing Chinese imports as a share of total imports is evident for glass and mineral wool. While the share of cement imports from China declined from 2006 to 2007, reliance on Chinese imports has also grown relative to 2002. According to representatives of the U.S. cement industry, Chinese production costs are between 20 percent and 40 percent of those in the United States.

Figure 9: Source of Imports Is Important for Trade Intensity

Share of 2007 total U.S. imports

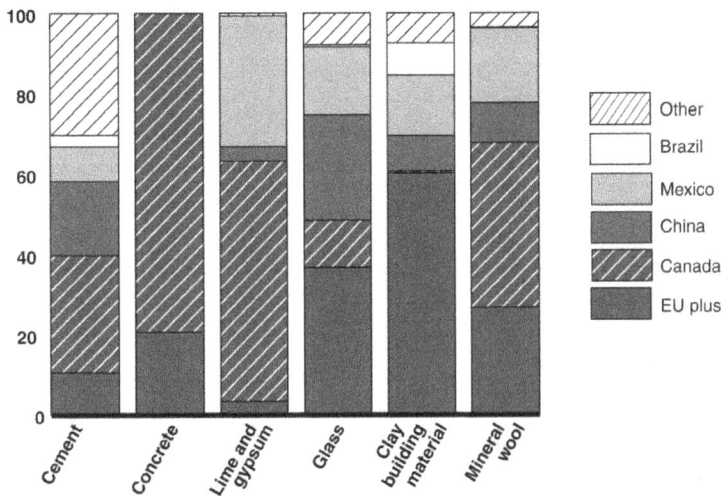

Legend: Other, Brazil, Mexico, China, Canada, EU plus

Source: GAO analysis of data from the Department of Commerce.

Notes to figure 9

Figure 10: Sub-Industries With Growing Share of Imports from China

Chinese imports as a share of total U.S. imports (percentage)

Glass — Mineral wool — Cement

Total U.S. imports by value (U.S. dollars in millions)						
Year	2002	2003	2004	2005	2006	2007
Cement	$938	924	1,140	1,567	1,837	1,325
Glass	$4,293	4,436	4,947	5,125	5,491	5,726
Mineral wool	$332	360	448	510	577	489

Source: GAO analysis of data from the Department of Commerce.

Notes to figure 10

Potentially Vulnerable Industries

PAPER PRODUCTS EXAMPLES

Sub-industry examples within paper products also show variation in energy and trade intensity. Pulp mills is the most trade intensive, at 98 percent. Paper mills is the largest sub-industry, with a 2007 value of output of over $51 billion and its trade intensity is 30 percent. Pulp mills and paper mills each has an energy intensity of 8 percent and, thus, meet both vulnerability criteria. While paperboard mills has an energy intensity of 12 percent, it does not meet the trade intensity criteria. Paperboard containers fails to meet both criteria but was the second largest sub-industry in 2007, with a value of output of over $47 billion.

Figure 11: Energy and Trade Intensity Indicators Vary by Sub-Industry

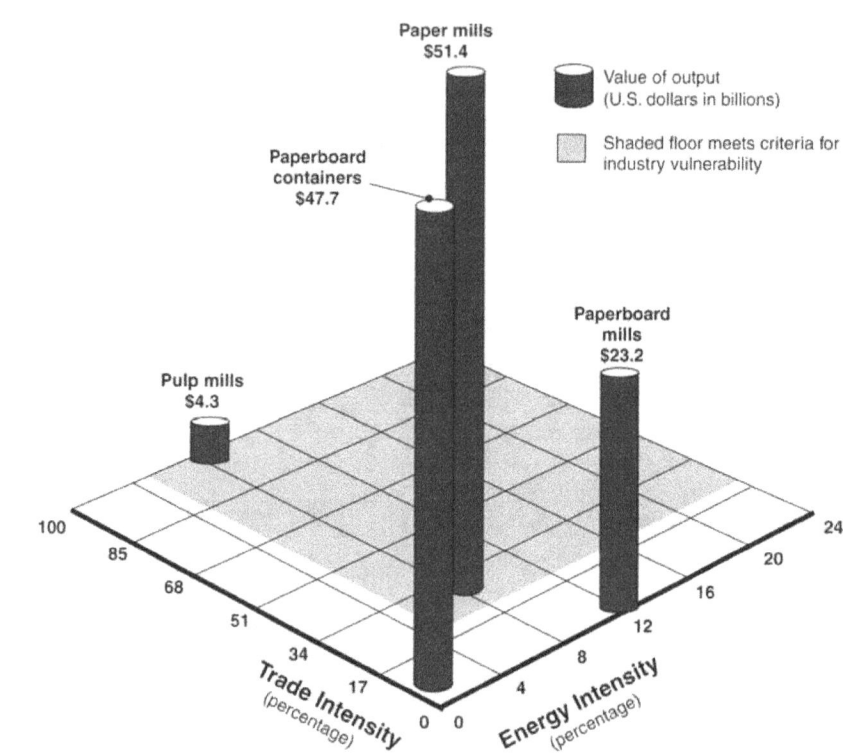

Source: GAO analysis of Department of Commerce energy data for 2006, output data for 2006 and 2007, and trade data for 2007.

Notes to figure 11

In paper mills and paperboard mills, the largest share of energy consumed is from the relatively less carbon-intensive renewable and other (such as fuel oil and steam) energy sources. An additional 20 percent of energy consumed is from natural gas, while coal and coke sources provide 14 percent of energy for paper mills and 9 percent of energy for paperboard mills. While energy use data for pulp mills is reported by the Department of Energy, consumption of coal and coke, specifically, is not publicly available, so percentage shares could not be computed. Data on energy use by paperboard containers are not currently reported.

Figure 12: Type of Energy Used Is Important for Carbon Intensity

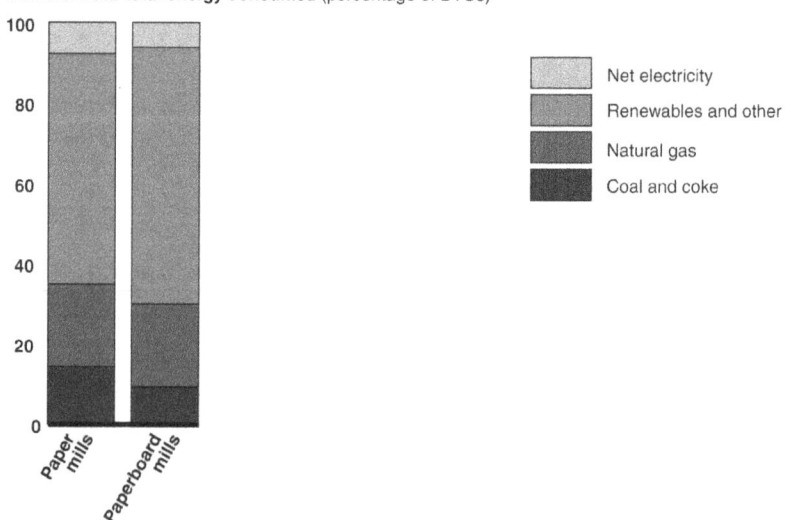

Source: GAO analysis of data from the Department of Energy.

Notes to figure 12

Potentially Vulnerable Industries

2.3

PAPER PRODUCTS EXAMPLES

For the paper products sub-industry examples, total imports exceed total exports. For each, the largest share of imports is from Canada, an Annex I country with agreed emission reduction targets. However, for the most trade-intensive example of pulp mills, 19 percent of imports are from Brazil. While paperboard containers has a trade intensity of only 6 percent, 27 percent of imports are from China.

Figure 13: Source of Imports Is Important for Trade Intensity

Share of 2007 total U.S. imports

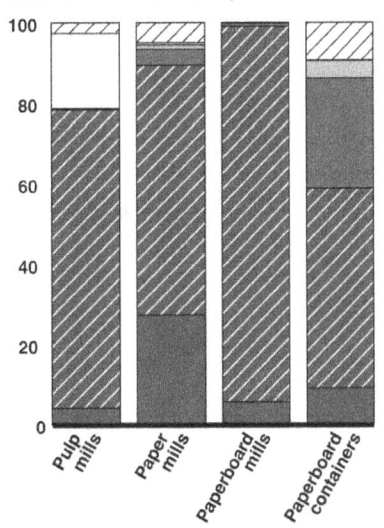

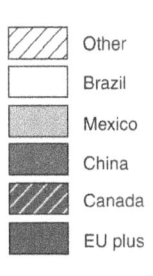

Source: GAO analysis of data from the Department of Commerce.

Among the paper products sub-industries, paperboard containers is the only example with a significant share of imports from China. While paperboard containers fails to meet the trade-intensity vulnerability criteria, emissions pricing could magnify the growing share of imports from China for that sub-industry. From 2002 to 2007, this share has grown from 11 percent to 27 percent of U.S. imports.

Figure 14: Sub-Industries With Growing Share of Imports from China

Chinese imports as a share of total U.S. imports (percentage)

Paperboard containers

Total U.S. imports by value (U.S. dollars in millions)						
Year	2002	2003	2004	2005	2006	2007
Paperboard container	$790	875	926	1,033	1,187	1,275

Source: GAO analysis of data from the Department of Commerce.

Notes to figure 14

Potentially Vulnerable Industries

2.4

CHEMICALS EXAMPLES

Among chemicals examples, alkalies and chlorine is the most energy intensive, at 26 percent, and nitrogenous fertilizers is the most trade intensive, at 82 percent. Except for industrial gases, each of the examples meets the energy and trade intensity criteria for vulnerability. Industrial gases, the largest sub-industry example, with a 2007 value of output of almost $9 billion, has an energy intensity of 15 percent but a trade intensity of only 5 percent. Not shown in figure 15 is petrochemicals, with a 2007 value of output of almost $62 billion. The Department of Commerce does not publicly provide energy-intensity data for petrochemicals, though industry experts estimate it to be at above 5 percent but below 20 percent. The year 2007 trade data indicate a petrochemicals trade intensity of below 15 percent.

Carbon black relies mostly on renewable and other sources of energy that are relatively less carbon intensive than coal. Nearly all of the energy consumed by nitrogenous fertilizers is from natural gas. In chemical sub-industries, a portion of the carbon contained in the energy source is also sequestered in the product rather than emitted to the atmosphere. Data on certain energy uses by type for sub-industries not shown in figure 16 is not publicly available and percentage shares could not be computed.

Figure 15: Energy and Trade Intensity Indicators Vary by Sub-Industry

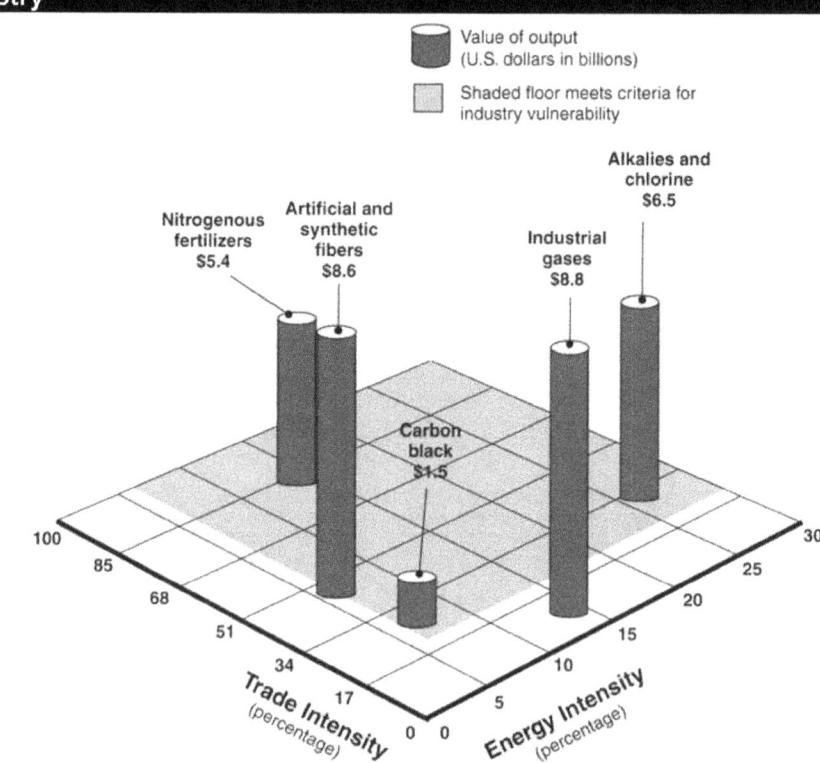

Source: GAO analysis of Department of Commerce energy data for 2006, output data for 2006 and 2007, and trade data for 2007.

Notes to figure 15

Figure 16: Type of Energy Used Is Important for Carbon Intensity

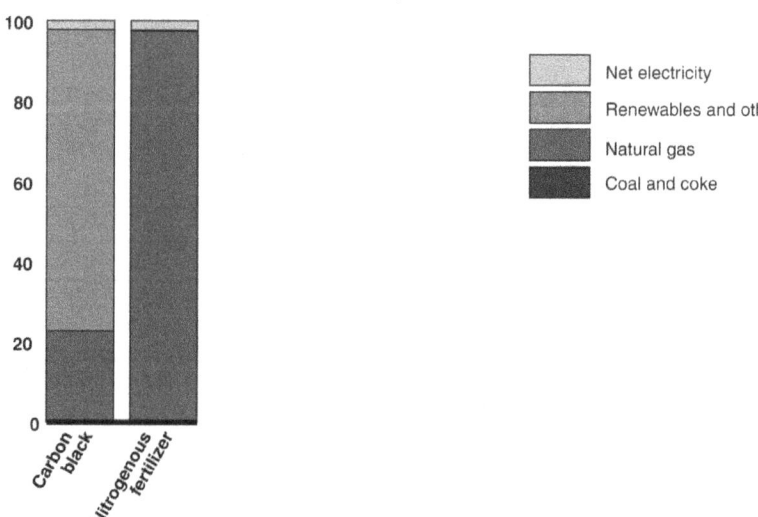

Source: GAO analysis of data from the Department of Energy.

Notes to figure 16

2.4

Potentially Vulnerable Industries

CHEMICALS EXAMPLES

For the chemicals examples, total imports exceed total exports. Nitrogenous fertilizers is the most trade intensive, and less than 40 percent of imports are from Annex I countries—Canada and EU Plus—while 40 percent of imports are from either Trinidad and Tobago or countries in the Middle East. Conversely, imports from Canada provide 60 percent of imports for carbon black. Imports from China, Mexico, and Korea account for 20 percent or more of imports in industrial gases and artificial and synthetic fibers.

Alkalies and chlorine is the only sub-industry example where exports comprise more than 60 percent of trade flows, with 15 percent to Brazil, 13 percent to Canada, and 12 percent to Mexico.

From 2002 to 2007, the share of imports from China has grown for alkalies and chlorine, industrial gases, and artificial and synthetic fibers from a share of less than 2 percent to a share of between 8 percent and 16 percent. According to representatives from the chemical industry, growing imports from China are also evident for industry downstream products, such as plastics.

Figure 17: Source of Imports Is Important for Trade Intensity

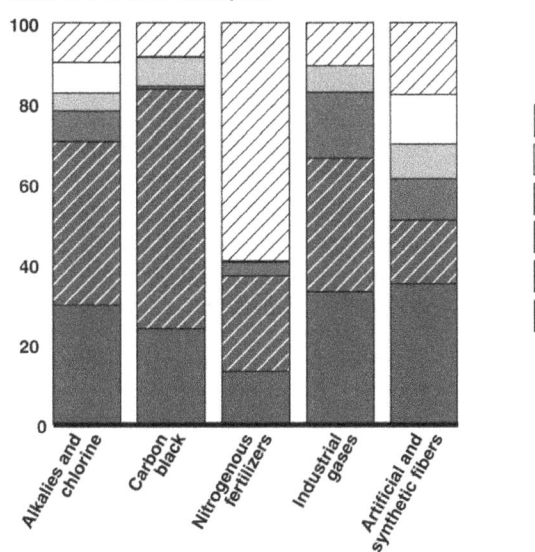

Source: GAO analysis of data from the Department of Commerce.

Notes to figure 17

Figure 18: Sub-Industries With Growing Share of Imports from China

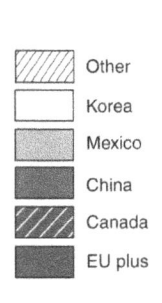

Total U.S. imports by value (U.S. dollars in millions)						
Year	2002	2003	2004	2005	2006	2007
Alkalies and chlorine	$160	207	253	454	460	400
Industrial gases	$125	128	148	160	160	176
Artifical and synthetic fibers	$1,626	1,644	1,814	2,230	2,322	2,471

Source: GAO analysis of data from the Department of Commerce.

Notes to figure 18

2.5

Potentially Vulnerable Industries

SUMMARY OF INDUSTRY EXAMPLES

This section provides data on energy and trade characteristics for sub-industries within primary metals, nonmetallic minerals, paper, and chemicals. As shown by the data, characteristics that contribute to an industry's or sub-industry's potential vulnerability to adverse competitiveness effects vary significantly among the examples provided. Additional variation would likely exist for factors not discussed, such as transportation costs and access to markets for natural resources, capital, and labor. As a result, the data provided are not sufficient to determine if one sub-industry is more vulnerable than another. Instead, the data suggest that an assessment of vulnerability that is based only on a sub-industry's energy and trade intensity may mask important differences in vulnerability among industries assessed.

- **Primary metals examples**: Primary aluminum is the most energy and trade intensive, yet the largest share of imports is from Canada. Iron and steel is the largest sub-industry that is both energy and trade intensive and also has the greatest reliance on coal and coke energy sources. Steel manufacturing and aluminum products fall short of meeting the trade-intensity criteria, but compared with the other examples, have the largest share of imports from China and the most pronounced trend of an increased import share from China since 2002.

- **Nonmetallic mineral examples**: Cement is the most energy intensive and has a relatively greater reliance on coal and coke energies. Glass is the most trade intensive and has the largest share of imports from China. Both cement and glass show an increasing share of Chinese imports since 2002. Concrete, while not meeting the trade-intensity criteria, exports more than it imports, with almost one-third of exports destined for markets in Mexico and the Middle East.

- **Paper examples**: Paper mills is the largest sub-industry example, although most imports are from Annex I countries. Almost one-fifth of pulp mill imports is from Brazil, although pulp mills is the smallest example that meets both energy and trade intensity criteria. Paperboard containers do not meet either vulnerability criteria, but show an increasing share of imports from China since 2002.

- **Chemicals examples**: Nitrogenous fertilizers is the most trade intensive, and 40 percent of imports are from Trinidad and Tobago or countries in the Middle East. Alkalies and chlorine are the most energy intensive and exports account for 79 percent of trade flows, of which, over one-fourth are to markets in Brazil and Mexico. Industrial gases do not meet either vulnerability criterion, but compared with the other examples, have the largest share of imports from China and the most pronounced trend of an increased import share from China since 2002.

Trade Measures

3

INTRODUCTION:

In this section, we discuss the use of trade measures and output-based rebates to address potential competitiveness and environmental effects of a domestic emissions pricing system. Through trade measures, such as a border tax adjustment or a border allowance requirement, international competitors without comparable climate policies would pay for greenhouse gas emissions associated with their exports to the United States. Output-based rebates have been proposed as another type of measure to offset the costs of climate policy for sectors that are exposed to unregulated competition through payments based on a per-unit government rebate or tax credit, or a per-unit allocation of emissions allowances.

How a trade measure is ultimately designed will have important implications for the effectiveness of the overall measure in addressing industry and environmental effects. In terms of output based rebates, the extent and design of the rebates could help address the industry effects, but could also affect the costs to other industries.

In this section we provide explanations of key features of trade and output-based measures included in climate change legislation introduced between April 2007 and June 2009. We also provide information on a range of views regarding the value of trade and output-based measures as policy tools to address competitiveness and environmental concerns. Additionally, we provide information on the potential implementation challenges associated with implementing these measures.

3.1

DIFFERENT TYPES

American Electric and Power Border Allowance Requirement

Some of the climate change bills introduced between April 2007 and June 2009 included provisions for a border allowance requirement. A border allowance requirement proposal was developed by the American Electric Power (AEP) and trade union representatives with the International Brotherhood of Electric Workers (IBEW). The AEP/IBEW proposal was introduced in July 2007 in S. 1766, 110TH Cong. (2007) and was also included in various other legislative proposals.

Trade measures have been proposed to address competitiveness and environmental effects associated with implementing a domestic emissions pricing system, such as a cap-and-trade system or a carbon tax system. Generally, in the context of a domestic emissions pricing system, trade measures would impose a cost or other requirement on energy-intensive imports from countries with weaker climate policies. Various types of trade measures exist for addressing competitiveness effects associated with a domestic emissions pricing system. Among the cap-and-trade and carbon tax legislative proposals we examined, border tax adjustments or border allowance requirements are the most frequently proposed type of trade measures.

Border Tax Adjustment

According to experts, a border tax adjustment is a levy applied by the federal government, on certain imported goods at the border. Key features of a border tax adjustment include the following:

- *Tax proportionate to the imports' embedded carbon*: Generally, the tax applied to the import would be based on the carbon emissions associated with the production of the imported good.

- *Tax equivalent to domestic compliance costs*: Generally, the federal government would charge imported goods the equivalent of what a domestic producer of a similar good would pay to comply with a domestic emissions pricing system.

Border Allowance Requirement

According to experts, a border allowance requirement is a measure that would require importers to purchase allowances from the federal government prior to importing goods into the United States. Generally, key features of a border allowance requirement include the following:

- *Establishes a separate pool of allowances*: In some of the cap-and-trade bills proposed in 2008, the federal government would establish a reserve of allowances separate from allowances established in the domestic cap-and-trade system. The border allowances that importers would be required to submit would come from this reserve allowance pool.

- *Comparable action determination*: Importers of goods from foreign countries that do not take "comparable action" to the United States to limit greenhouse gas emissions, would be required to submit allowances to accompany exports to the United States of the covered good.

- *Documentation at the border*: Prior to entering the United States, importers would have to purchase allowances from the federal government, and submit a written declaration at the border stating that the good is accompanied by the required number of allowances. Generally, the number of allowances required would be proportionate to the embedded carbon content of the import.

Trade Measures

3.1

SUPPORTERS' VIEWS

Some policy analysts, industry stakeholders, climate change experts, and government officials argue that trade measures help address competitiveness and environmental effects associated with domestic emissions pricing systems. For example, some supporters contend that trade measures may do the following:

- *Prevent a decline in output by U.S. producers*: Trade measures would help level the playing field by imposing similar costs on imports from countries without comparable carbon mitigation policies. The potential exists for certain U.S. firms to lose business to energy-intensive imports from countries with weaker climate policies. Moreover, firms could further lose international competitiveness due to the indirect costs of purchasing more expensive U.S. energy. As a result, U.S. firms in vulnerable industries could suffer a loss in output, profits, and employment.

- *Prevent carbon leakage*: Trade measures would prevent U.S. energy-intensive industries from shifting production to countries without comparable carbon mitigation policies, resulting in carbon leakage, where emission reductions in the United States are replaced to some degree by production and emission growth in less regulated countries. Supporters of trade measures stated that carbon leakage could lead to higher volumes of greenhouse gas emissions worldwide.

- *Create leverage on other countries to reduce emissions:* Trade measures would create incentives for major trading partners to adopt similar climate policies. For example, proponents of trade measures argue that trade measures could potentially provide leverage to U.S. climate negotiators in their efforts to establish a global framework that includes other major emitting nations. Some industry stakeholders with whom we spoke, for example, stated that the potential benefit of a trade measure in increasing pressure on developing countries may trump its adverse economic effects. These stakeholders said that countries' statements of opposition to proposed trade measures provided evidence of their effectiveness in providing leverage.

- *Political acceptability*: If a climate change bill is to pass, it will be necessary that the bill include a provision like a trade measure to address competitiveness effects. Policy experts stated that most climate change proposals with trade measures have garnered support from industries that could be affected by a domestic emissions pricing system.

Trade Measures

3.1

OPPONENTS' VIEWS

Some policy analysts, climate change experts, and government officials raise concerns that trade measures may motivate retaliatory actions, undermine efforts to secure multilateral consensus, and generate little leverage. For example, some opponents contend that trade measures may do the following:

- *Motivate retaliatory action*: An important implication of U.S. trade measures is how they would be perceived by other countries and impact negotiations aimed toward an international climate agreement. Opponents argued that trade measures could be viewed by other countries as an antagonistic step, and could lead to retaliatory action from other countries.

- *Undermine efforts to secure international consensus*: While there is general agreement that the global scope of the climate change problem will require actions from all major emitting nations, there are differing views on the impact that trade measures may have in securing an international consensus. Foreign government officials with whom we spoke, declined to give formal positions on trade measure proposals given that a climate change bill has not yet passed Congress. But some officials expressed concerns over the unilateral application of a trade measure by the United States and said that competitiveness effects would be better addressed through multilateral discussions. Because multilateral approaches involve commitments to reduce greenhouse gas emissions by more than one country, they also level the playing field. Multilateral approaches include international agreements, such as the Kyoto Protocol, or international action, as when countries independently decide to reduce their emissions of greenhouse gases. Multilateral approaches may involve sectoral agreements, leveling the playing field worldwide within an industry. Foreign embassy officials also stated that trade measures are not likely to be effective tool to leverage other countries to take steps to reduce emissions and that a unilateral U.S. trade measure could add to the challenge of developing multilateral consensus on climate change mitigation efforts.

Trade Measures

3.1 OPPONENTS' VIEWS

- *Generate little leverage on other countries to reduce emissions:* The effectiveness of trade measures in creating leverage on foreign countries to reduce emissions will vary with the share of their output that is imported into the United States compared with the share that is consumed domestically or exported to other countries. In addition, some policy experts we spoke to note that in some cases, the emission costs that foreign firms will have to pay on their imports into the United States may not be sufficient to motivate them to change domestic production processes. For example, in each of the vulnerable industries listed in table 2, less than 1 percent of total Chinese output is imported into the United States, although the share may be higher for individual firms. Instead, most of the Chinese output in these industries is consumed domestically or in countries that may or may not impose a domestic emissions pricing system. Nonetheless, in certain cases, a U.S. trade measure may be effective in providing some degree of leverage. For example, U.S. iron and steel imports represent more than 8 percent of output in Brazil and more than 10 percent of output in Mexico. In addition, U.S. imports of nitrogenous fertilizers from the Middle East are more than 20 percent of production from that region.

Table 2: U.S. Imports as a Share of Foreign Output (percentage of metric tons)

	Iron and steel	Primary aluminum	Cement	Pulp products	Nitrogenous fertilizers
Brazil	8.3	5.0	1.1	10.8	3.5
China	0.5	0.3	0.9	0.1	0.5
India	0.7	0.0	0.0	n/a	0.0
Mexico	10.6	n/a	5.6	1.1	8.3
Middle East	0.1	6.5	0.2	0.0	22.1

Source: GAO analysis of production data from the U.S. Geological Survey and the Food and Agriculture Organization and trade data from the Department of Commerce.

Notes to Table
Data are for 2007, except for cement and nitrogenous fertilizers with data for 2006.
Iron and steel production figures include those for pig iron, direct-reduced iron, and raw steel.
Cement production figures are for hydraulic cement.
Pulp products production figures represent the total for "pulp for paper" products within FAOSTAT.
Nitrogenous fertilizer production figures represent tonnage by total nutrients within FAOSTAT.
Not included in the iron and steel import figures above were about 38 million liters from Mexico.

Trade Measures

3.1

IMPLEMENTATION CHALLENGES

Trade measures could present implementation challenges, particularly with obtaining necessary data to measure the carbon content of imports, and to evaluate and assess climate change actions of other countries. Examples of potential implementation challenges include the following:

- *Determining the embedded carbon content in imports*: Generally, imposing a trade measure on an import would require a determination of the embedded carbon content, or the amount of greenhouse gases emitted during the production of the imported good. According to experts, accurately measuring the embedded carbon content for specific items would be challenging. Furthermore, climate policy experts point out that while determining the embedded carbon content in standardized products like steel, primary aluminum, and basic chemicals would be difficult, it would be even more challenging to assess the embedded carbon content of products that rely on these goods for final assembly.

  Additionally, climate policy experts noted that, variations in the type of energy used can result in different carbon intensities for goods that appear identical at the border. To accurately assess the embedded carbon content of a product, the administrator of the program would be required to obtain specific plant-level information on the production process of the import from foreign countries.

  Accurately measuring the embedded carbon content of an import would require significant data, resulting in several data reliability concerns with obtaining carbon data from international inventories. Experts and industry stakeholders alike reported that obtaining data from foreign producers could be a challenge, and that using data from international inventories could raise several data reliability concerns as the United States would have no way of verifying that the data obtained was accurate. In addition, under the S. 3036 110TH Cong. (2008), importers would have to submit a declaration statement at the border declaring the imported good is accompanied by the required number of allowances. Agency officials we spoke to noted that officials would not know if the information contained in the declaration was accurate.

- *Evaluating and assessing climate change actions*: As previously discussed, a key feature of a trade measure provision is the requirement of determining the comparability of other countries' actions to address climate change. According to policy experts, among some of the cap-and-trade bills introduced, some have not clearly defined or assessed the method for determining how other countries' actions on climate change would be assess by the U.S. government. In order for the implementing agency to assess the comparability of different countries, the criteria for making this determination would have to be defined either in the legislation or implementing regulations.

Trade Measures

3.1

DESIGN TRADE-OFFS

In designing a trade measure, there are a range of possible options to consider as illustrated in table 3. The design features of trade measures involve different trade-offs that will have implications for the effectiveness of the overall measure in addressing competitiveness and environmental concerns.

For example, a key design consideration is the timing for when the trade measure would go into effect. Delaying the implementation of the trade measure could result in the measure being a more effective leverage tool because it would provide other countries with an opportunity to implement similar carbon mitigation policies. On the other hand, industry stakeholders with whom we spoke argued that a delay in implementing the trade measure could adversely affect U.S. industries by incurring costs under a domestic emissions pricing system that their foreign competitors would not face. According to some stakeholders, this could result in U.S. industries being at a competitive disadvantage compared to foreign competitors.

The method for determining the comparability of other countries' actions also involves important trade-offs. Given the different approaches being utilized to address climate change, questions have been raised over whether these different actions would be deemed comparable to U.S. efforts. Industry groups have argued that the method for determining comparability should be based on quantitative criteria that are equivalent to criteria U.S. producers must meet. However, providing flexibility on determining comparability allows countries to utilize the approach best suited for reducing emissions in their individual country.

Table 3: Policy Experts Cite Trade-offs Involved in the Design of Trade Measures

Feature	Options	Design trade-offs
Date when the trade measure goes into effect	The trade measure can go into effect simultaneously when a domestic cap-and-trade system goes into effect or at a later date.	Having the trade measure go into effect simultaneously when the domestic cap-and-trade system goes into effect may reduce impacts on U.S. industry competitiveness. Delaying the implementation of the trade measure allows time for international climate negotiations and for countries to take action on reducing their emissions.
Type of products covered	Climate bills in the 110th Congress limited coverage of the trade measure to specified products such as importers of steel, aluminum, and cement; whereas other bills expanded coverage to manufactured goods that met eligibility criteria.	Limiting product coverage may exclude industries vulnerable to competitiveness effects. Expanding product coverage increases federal challenges to track emissions
Defining comparable action	Proposals have varied in stringency and level of detail in outlining the methodology for determining comparable action.	Quantitative criteria for assessing comparable action may not measure the level of effort on climate policy that a country actually undertakes. Flexibility and discretion on comparability determinations increases uncertainty for industry stakeholders.
Calculating border allowance requirements	Proposals have varied in the level of detail in outlining the methodology for calculating the number of allowances industries will be required to submit at the border. Earlier proposals based border allowance requirements on averages for country industry sectors; H.R. 2454 delegated the decision to the future implementing agency.	Basing border allowance requirements on industry average increases implementation feasibility as firm-level data likely not available. Using industry average for baseline may limit incentives to improve efficiency and would penalize efficient firms.

Source: GAO analysis of selected climate change legislation introduced between April 2007 and June 2009 that included trade measures.

Trade Measures

3.2

ALTERNATIVE: OUTPUT-BASED REBATES

Output-based rebates have been proposed as policy alternatives to using trade measures. These rebates would be provided to energy-intensive (or greenhouse gas-intensive) and trade-exposed industries to cover their increased costs from the carbon pricing system. Under legislative proposals, EPA would determine the average energy (or greenhouse gas) intensity per unit of production for each relevant industrial sector and then distribute allowances based on each facility's amount of production. Although some industry stakeholders note that output-based rebates address competitiveness effects by compensating covered firms for incurred costs, some climate policy experts note that output-based rebates could distort pricing, could reduce incentives for firms to engage in conservation, and may drive up the cost of the program.

Output-based Rebates

Output-based rebates are measures designed to financially rebate industries for the costs incurred under a domestic emissions pricing system. According to policy experts, key features of an output-based rebate include the following:

- *Tied to firm's level of output*: Generally, output-based rebates would be tied to a firm's level of output. For example, firms that expand their operations will receive a larger rebate, while firms that downsize but continue to produce in the United States will receive a smaller rebate. Firms that move offshore or shut down would receive no rebate. A rebate can take the form of a per-unit rebate or tax credit, or a per-unit allocation of emissions allowances.

- *Compensates for incurred costs*: For a facility with an average level of energy intensity (or greenhouse gas intensity) these rebates would cover both direct and indirect costs. These would include their own emissions and costs associated with higher energy prices and technology purchases to improve energy efficiency. Providing allowances based on average industry intensity, energy intensity and production levels, rather than providing them based on each firm's historical emissions, is intended to reward the most efficient facilities and create an incentive for continued efficiency improvements.

H.R. 2454 111th Cong. (2009) included provisions for output-based rebates to offset the costs incurred by firms to comply with a cap-and-trade system. Two other climate change bills, H.R. 7146, 110th Cong. (2008) and H.R. 1759, 111th Cong. (2009), also incorporated output-based rebates. In all three proposals, allowances would be distributed among certain energy- and trade- intensive industries according to an individual firm's output.

3.2

ALTERNATIVE: OUTPUT-BASED REBATES

Supporters' Views

Some policy analysts, climate change experts, and government officials argue that output-based rebates may address some of the limitations associated with using trade measures. For example, some supporters contend that output-based rebates may do the following:

- *Mitigate costs incurred by U.S. producers*: Output-based rebates are necessary to compensate U.S. firms for costs incurred while complying with a domestic emissions pricing system. Supporters note that trade measures only apply costs to foreign competitors at the border, while output-based rebates affect producers' costs for both domestic and export markets. Among the key supporters of output-based rebates are stakeholders in energy-intensive industries who note that energy costs are a substantial portion of their manufacturing costs. According to these stakeholders, proposals that mitigate costs at the production level, either by allocating free allowances to qualifying facilities or rebating the costs of allowances offsets the disincentive created by higher energy prices in the United States.

- *Reward efficient firms*: Output-based rebates are generally allocated in proportion to current levels of production rather than being fixed to historical measures. Supporters argue that because the rebates or allocations are tied to production levels, individual firms have an incentive to increase their production. According to supporters, rebates reward the most productive plants and stimulate investments in efficient technology. Moreover, the rebates would benefit firms that face competition from foreign suppliers in markets at home or global export markets or both.

- *Use U.S. data*: Implementing output-based rebates may be more manageable than implementing trade measures. For example, in proposed legislation, agencies would only require data from U.S. data sources to identify firms that would be eligible for output-based rebates. This differs from trade measures which would require data from foreign firms' production, which could be more difficult to obtain. In addition, legislative proposals have generally been explicit about the U.S. data sources and criteria to be used in identifying eligible industries.

Trade Measures

3.2

ALTERNATIVE: OUTPUT-BASED REBATES

Opponents' Views

Some policy analysts, climate change experts, and government officials argue that despite several advantages identified with using output-based rebates, several potential limitations also exist. For example, some opponents contend that output-based rebates offset the costs of climate policy for sectors that are exposed to unregulated competition, and thereby lower the incentives for those firms to engage in conservation and reduce their energy intensity. Similarly, output-based rebates would likely result in relatively lower output prices for the products produced by firms receiving rebates, thereby reducing the incentives for consumers of those products to conserve. Moreover, some climate policy experts argue that output-based rebates create a subsidy for certain energy-intensive industries which would require non energy-intensive firms to engage in greater efforts to reduce the emissions intensity of their production.

Potential Implementation Challenges

Although the data requirements for an output-based measure may be more manageable than those of a trade measure, some challenges related to identifying electricity distribution data exist. For example, under HR 2454, 111th Cong. (2009), EPA would be required to obtain production data on various commodities from energy-intensive industries, including electricity distribution data. Data on electricity use on a facility-by-facility basis is not currently collected by government agencies. Provisions in either the legislation or in implementing regulations would have to be explicit on how to obtain data on electricity use.

Additionally, according to EPA officials, the methodology outlined in HR 2454, 111th Cong. (2009), for how to determine eligible industries does not align with data that would be collected under EPA's proposed mandatory greenhouse gas reporting rule. According to climate policy experts, standard mechanisms for reviewing eligibility for the rebates are needed to ensure that the policy does not over compensate certain industries.

3.3

Between April 2007 and June 2009, several cap-and-trade and carbon tax bills were introduced with provisions to address the potential competitiveness and environmental effects of implementing a domestic emissions pricing system. For example, of the cap-and-trade bills that we examined and that were introduced during that period, some included trade measures such as an allowance requirement at the border or a border tax.

As illustrated in figure 19, two bills introduced in 2009 have included provisions for using output-based rebates. The most recent bill, H.R. 2454, 111th Cong. (2009) includes a provision for output-based rebates. Under that bill, energy intensive and trade exposed industries would receive allowances to cover their increased costs.

Several industry stakeholders with whom we spoke, reported that output-based rebates and trade measures could function as complimentary measures to address competitiveness concerns. For example, in H.R. 2454, 111th Cong. (2009), the output-based rebates would be phased out by 2035 unless the President decides to extend them. In that bill, the trade measure would go into effect after 2020, unless the President determines it would not be in the national interest and Congress passes an affirmative joint resolution within 90 days.

Some stakeholders have stated that having the trade measure to go into effect at a later time may provide time for the United States to be part of international negotiations on climate change.

Trade Measures

LEGISLATIVE HISTORY OF TRADE MEASURES AND OUTPUT-BASED REBATES

Figure 19: Proposals Move toward Using Output-Based Rebates to Address Competitiveness Concerns

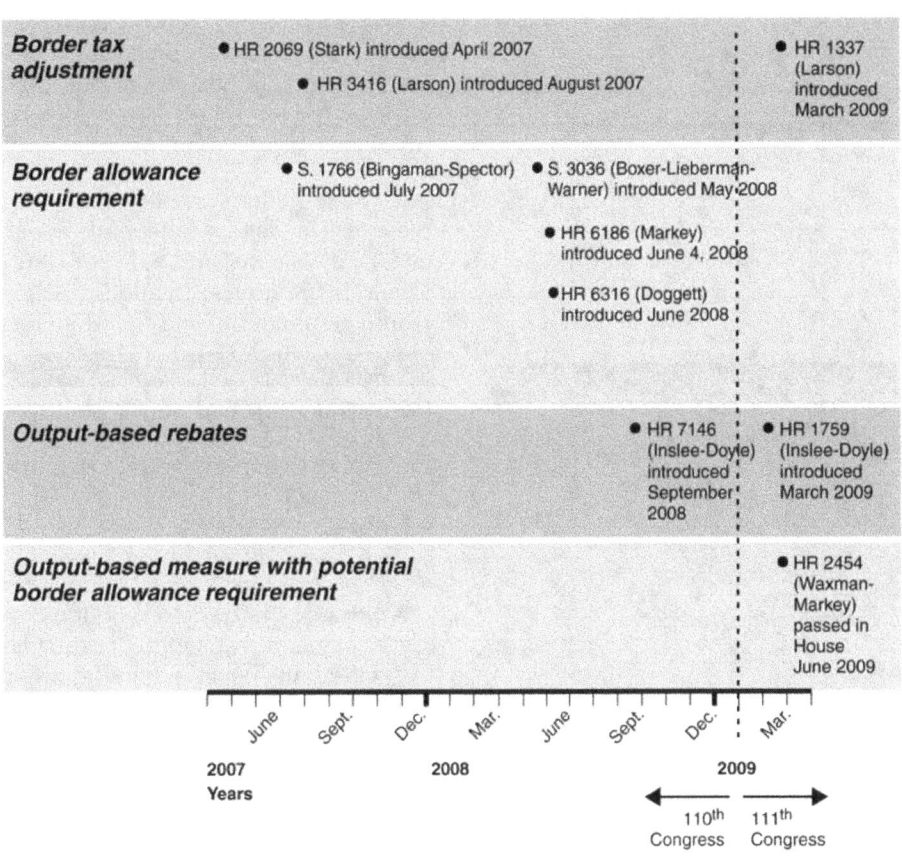

Source: GAO analysis.

Notes to figure 19

International Trade Implications

OVERVIEW

4

INTRODUCTION:

In this section, we discuss potential international implications of a U.S. trade measure, such as concerns about countries possibly retaliating in response to a trade measure or its potential impact on the multilateral trading system. In addition, we provide information on the WTO dispute settlement process, a forum that facilitates the resolution of specific trade disputes. We provide information on the WTO provisions and key questions that may apply if a U.S. trade measure or an output-based rebate were to be challenged at the WTO.

Assessing the international trade implications is difficult for a number of reasons. One is that it depends in part upon how other nations reduce their carbon emissions, and whether they perceive any U.S. measures as likely to affect their exports. In addition, the outcome of a WTO challenge, if any, would be uncertain and may depend on how the measure is implemented.

Potential Bilateral and Multilateral Trade Impacts

According to experts and foreign officials we spoke with, U.S. climate change trade measures may have implications for U.S. and multilateral trade relations.

- *Potential for bilateral trade retaliation:* Countries may view U.S. trade measures as trade restrictions or sanctions, which could lead them to implement restrictions against U.S. exports. Other countries could potentially develop counter measures based on a different test of "comparability," such as historical or per capita emissions, according to trade experts we spoke with.

  Although no other country has yet to implement a trade measure based on greenhouse gas emissions, European officials have previously considered the use of trade measures on countries, including the United States, that have not taken actions that match European standards. In addition, support within other countries for imposing trade measures could increase if the United States implements a trade measure.

- *Potential for increased trade tensions:* A broader concern is that escalating retaliation between the United States and other countries could lead to significant global trade tensions. Given the volume of trade in goods that could potentially be affected by trade measures linked to greenhouse gas emissions, some officials and experts have argued that escalating tensions and responses to these measures could ultimately do significant harm to the functioning of the multilateral trading system under the WTO. Trade experts told us that trade measures and responses could potentially pose systemic challenges to the WTO and its dispute resolution system. For example, multiple challenges brought up by other countries based on different imported products could tie up the system.

International Trade Implications

4.1

WTO COMPLIANCE QUESTIONS

WTO Dispute Settlement Process

Consultation (up to 60 days)

Panel Review (generally up to 6 months, but in no case more than 9 months)

Appellate Stage (60 to 90 days)

DSB Decision (generally up to 9 months and up to 12 months if the panel report is appealed)

Implementation Stage (if immediate compliance is impractical, member given a 'reasonable period of time' to comply, which normally should not exceed 15 months from adoption of report up to 15 months)

A unilateral U.S. trade measure or system of rebates linked to a climate change policy may be challenged by other countries through the WTO's dispute resolution process. Countries could potentially raise different types of challenges depending on the design of the trade measure or rebate, and several key questions may be relevant in the consideration of a WTO dispute. These questions stem from the WTO provisions under which the trade measures or rebates may be challenged and reviewed, including the General Agreement on Tariffs and Trade (GATT), and the Agreement on Subsidies and Countervailing Duties (ASCM).

The following pages describe in more detail the questions, factors, and WTO provisions listed in table 4.

WTO Dispute Settlement Process

The WTO's dispute settlement system facilitates the resolution of specific trade disputes and serves as a vehicle for upholding trade rules and preserving the rights and obligations of WTO Members under WTO agreements. WTO Members may request consultations concerning measures affecting the operation of such WTO agreements. After consultations, WTO Members can request the establishment of a panel to hear their claims regarding alleged inconsistencies of other Member's measures. The panel will issue a report of its findings, which will be adopted by the WTO Dispute Settlement Body (DSB), unless a party to the dispute appeals the panel's report, which is reviewed by the WTO Appellate Body. WTO disputes can take several years or more to complete the entire process. If the responding party does not prevail and fails to comply with the rulings and recommendations of the DSB, the complaining party may seek authority to suspend concessions or other obligations under the WTO agreements.

Table 4: Key Questions That May be Considered in a WTO Challenge		
Key questions	**Discussion**	**WTO provisions**
1. Is the trade measure consistent with WTO market access requirements?	Customs duties or other duties or charges on imports in excess of schedules of concessions may not be imposed. Subject to exceptions, prohibitions or restrictions, other than duties, taxes or other charges, on imports may not be imposed.	GATT Article II, XI
2. Is the trade measure consistent with WTO non-discrimination requirements?	Measure must treat imported products no less favorably than like domestic products.	GATT Article III
	Measure must also not discriminate among goods from different countries.	GATT Article I
3. If not WTO consistent, is the trade measure covered by a WTO environmental exception?	Measure relating to conservation of exhaustible natural resources or that is necessary to protect human, animal or plant health is covered under WTO exceptions.	GATT Article XX (b), (g)
	To be covered, measure must not be applied in a manner which would constitute a means of arbitrary or unjustifiable discrimination or be a disguised restriction on international trade	GATT Article XX chapeau
4. Are output-based rebates consistent with WTO rules governing subsidies?	The rebates must not involve a specific subsidy or other benefit that causes adverse effects to other WTO Members.	ASCM

Source: GAO analysis of legal scholars' views on questions and provisions that may be relevant in analyzing trade measures contained in climate change legislation for consistency with WTO rules.

International Trade Implications

4.1

WTO COMPLIANCE

The following observations are based on comments from various legal scholars and other non-governmental commentators on questions and provisions that may be relevant in analyzing trade measures contained in climate change legislation for consistency with WTO rules.

1. Is the Trade Measure Consistent with WTO Market Access Rules and Commitments?

An initial question involves how a trade measure would be interpreted and the corresponding GATT article under which the measure would be reviewed.

- GATT Article II:1(b) prohibits a WTO Member from applying customs duties or other duties or charges to imports in excess of the Member's schedule of tariff concessions.

- GATT Article XI:1 prohibits prohibitions or restrictions, other than duties, taxes or other charges, on imports, with certain exceptions.

- According to legal experts, a "border tax" imposed on imports equivalent to a tax imposed on like domestic products may be WTO compliant.

2. Is the Trade Measure Consistent with WTO Non-Discrimination Requirements?

Trade measures must also be consistent with WTO non-discrimination provisions covering most favored nation status treatment and national treatment.

- *Does a trade measure treat two like products differently depending on country of origin?* GATT Article I:1 provides, in part, that with respect to customs duties and charges imposed on or in connection with importation and exportation, and the method of levying such duties and charges, any advantage granted by any WTO Member to any product originating in any other Member is to be accorded immediately and unconditionally to the like product originating in or destined for all other WTO Members.

- *Does a trade measure treat imported products less favorably than like domestic products?* GATT Article III:4 provides, in part, that imported products shall be accorded treatment no less favorable than that accorded to like products of national origin in respect of all laws, regulations, and requirements affecting their internal sale, offering for sale, purchase, transportation, distribution, or use.

4.1

Shrimp-Turtle Case - In this 1996 case, four WTO members challenged as discriminatory a U.S. embargo on the importation of certain shrimp and shrimp products from countries that had not been certified by the Department of State as having a comprehensive sea turtle conservation regime. The United States argued that the measure was justified under article XX (g).

However, the WTO panel found, in part, that the U.S. measure was not justified under article XX (g) because it met the panel's test of being a "risk to the multilateral trading system." Upon appeal, the Appellate Body rejected the panel's test and found that the measure fell within article XX (g). However, the Appellate Body also found the U.S. measure had been applied in an arbitrary and discriminatory manner.

The United States was ultimately able to comply with WTO rulings by making changes in the way the law was administered, including revising guidelines to establish greater transparency and due process in country certification decisions.

International Trade Implications

WTO COMPLIANCE

3. If the Trade Measure Is Not Permissible Under Core WTO Obligations, Would it Be Covered Under an Environmental Exception?

If a trade measure does not comply with GATT market access or non-discrimination provisions, it may still be justified under certain GATT environmental exceptions. A key consideration would be the interpretation of the intended purpose of the measure and whether it is designed to serve an environmental objective.

- *Is the trade measure designed to serve an environmental objective?*

  o GATT Article XX (b) provides an exception for measures necessary to protect human, animal, or plant life or health.

  o GATT Article XX (g) provides an exception for measures relating to the conservation of exhaustible natural resources if such measures are made effective in conjunction with restrictions on domestic production or consumption.

- *How is the measure applied?* The introduction (chapeau) to GATT Article XX states that such measures must not be applied in a manner that would constitute a means of arbitrary or unjustifiable discrimination or a disguised restriction on international trade.

4. Are Output-Based Rebates Consistent with WTO Rules Governing Subsidies?

The ASCM imposes disciplines on certain kinds of subsidies to domestic producers, such as those that cause adverse effects to foreign competitors.

- *Is an output-based rebate or distribution of free allowances a subsidy?* To be considered a subsidy under the ASCM, a system of rebates would need to involve (1) a "financial contribution" by the government or any form of income or price support that (2) confers a "benefit" to the recipient and (3) is "specific."

- *Is the rebate an "actionable" subsidy that causes "adverse effects" to the interests of other WTO Members?* A further key question is whether a rebate, if found to be a subsidy, would cause "serious prejudice" to the interests of other WTO Members.

Appendix 1

OBJECTIVES, SCOPE, AND METHODOLOGY

Our research objectives were to examine: (1) information on estimating industry effects; (2) examples of industries that may be vulnerable to a loss in international competitiveness from emissions pricing; (3) trade measures and other approaches to address competitiveness issues; and (4) potential international implications of trade measures.

To address all of these objectives, we (1) reviewed relevant climate change academic literature and federal agency documents; (2) reviewed and analyzed studies and data on climate change from a variety of sources, including past GAO work, the U.S. Census Bureau and Departments of Commerce and Energy, international organizations, policy institutes, and universities; (3) interviewed agency officials from the Office of the U.S. Trade Representative (USTR); the Environmental Protection Agency (EPA); the Departments of Commerce, State, Energy, and Treasury, and the Department of Homeland Security's Customs and Border Protection (CBP); (4) conducted interviews with subject-matter experts selected from a population of individuals from government, academia, business, and professional organizations. Several criteria were used for selecting experts to interview including: type and depth of experience, the expert's recognition in the professional community, relevance of published work, professional affiliations, present and past positions held, and other subject matter experts' recommendations.

Objective 1 and 2:

To better understand how implementing a domestic emissions pricing system would likely affect the international competitiveness of U.S industries, we reviewed relevant studies from GAO, EPA, the Department of Energy's Energy Information Agency (EIA), and international organizations. We also reviewed documents and interviewed experts from policy institutes, universities, and industry.

Recently proposed legislation identifies industries potentially vulnerable to adverse competitiveness effects as those with: (a) either energy intensity or greenhouse gas intensity of 5 percent or greater; and (b) a trade intensity of 15 percent or greater.[1] Since calculation of greenhouse gas intensity requires an emissions price—not yet determined—and detailed industry data on greenhouse gas emissions—not currently available—we focus our analysis on industry energy intensity. However, energy intensity is also an imperfect measure of potential vulnerability since energy use is not the only source of industrial greenhouse gas emissions, and an industry's energy expenditures may rise with to a change in market prices, even if the industry's greenhouse emissions decline. Additionally, many factors may determine the vulnerability of any particular firm, including transportation costs, supply chain relationships, and access to markets for natural resources, capital, or labor.

---

[1] For example, H.R. 2454 (111th Cong.), and H.R. 1759 (111th Cong.) include these criteria. HR 2454 also identifies industries with an energy intensity of 20 percent or greater as vulnerable to adverse competitiveness effects irrespective of trade intensity; however, none of the examples we discuss in our analysis would be identified as vulnerable under these criteria.

Appendix 1

OBJECTIVES, SCOPE, AND METHODOLOGY

Based on industry and expert studies, most industries that meet both vulnerability criteria are within primary metals, nonmetallic minerals, paper products, and chemicals.[2] Quantitative analysis of the estimated competitiveness impacts of U.S. greenhouse gas emissions pricing is relatively limited. We present results for two studies that separate the international competitiveness effects from U.S. emissions pricing from the domestic market effects. Estimated results from these two studies include findings that are broadly consistent with those of other studies. For example, a study of climate policy impacts on U.S. industries was commissioned by the National Committee on Energy Policy and studies of the European Union's climate policies have been performed for the European Commission and the International Energy Agency. In each of these studies, the list of vulnerable industries is generally consistent, as is the finding that estimated impacts could be greater for energy-intensive industries.

To illustrate variation in economic characteristics among these four manufacturing industries, we analyzed: (1) energy consumption data from the U.S. Census Bureau's Annual Survey of Manufacturers; (2) energy use data from EIA's Manufacturing Energy Consumption Survey; (3) international trade data from the Department of Commerce's International Trade Administration; and (4) U.S. and international production data from the Department of Commerce's Bureau of Economic Analysis, the U.S. Geological Survey and the United Nations Food and Agricultural Organization (FAO). For analysis of sub-industries, we examined data with a Census Bureau North American Industry Classification System (NAICS) code of 5 to 6 digits, depending on how the data were reported in each of the databases reviewed and for consistency of comparison with other studies. For the vulnerable sub-industry charts, we applied multiple criteria to show variation in industry characteristics of energy intensity, trade intensity, and primary trading partners. For example, we selected sub-industries that met both the energy and trade intensity criteria, examples that met only one criterion, and examples that met neither, but had significant imports from non-Annex I countries. We do not identify the complete list of potentially vulnerable sub-industries, a list that will vary depending on the level of aggregation in product lines that is examined. The specific list of example sub-industries we selected, along with their corresponding NAICS codes can be found in table 5.

---

[2] A study commissioned by energy-intensive industries identifies 41 manufacturing sub-industries as meeting these vulnerability criteria in at least one year between 2004 and 2006, of which 34 sub-industries are within primary metals, nonmetallic minerals, paper products, and chemicals. We did not conduct sensitivity analysis to determine how many additional sub-industries would be identified as vulnerable if the criteria were defined more broadly. According to another expert, the list of potentially vulnerable sub-industries is greater if using the proposed energy-intensive criteria compared with carbon-intensity criteria using a per ton carbon price of $20 or $30. Further, eliminating the trade-intensity criteria would mean that roughly an additional 10 sub-industries would be identified as vulnerable, whereas eliminating the energy-intensity criteria would yield over 150 sub-industries that would be identified as vulnerable to competitiveness effects.

Appendix 1

OBJECTIVES, SCOPE, AND METHODOLOGY

Table 5: Sub-Industries Selected as Vulnerable Industry Examples

Sub-Industry Examples	North American Industry Classification System Codes
Primary Metals	331
Iron and steel mills	331111
Electrometallurgical products	331112
Steel manufacturing	33121, 33122
Ferrous metal foundries	33151
Primary aluminum	331312
Aluminum products	331314, 331316
Nonmetallic Minerals	327
Cement	32731
Concrete	32732
Lime and gypsum	3274
Glass	32721
Clay building material	32712
Mineral wool	327993
Paper Products	322
Pulp mills	32211
Paper mills	32212
Paperboard mills	32213
Paperboard containers	32221
Chemicals	325
Alkalies and chlorine	325181
Carbon black	325182
Nitrogenous fertilizers	325311
Industrial gases	32512
Artificial and synthetic fibers	32522

Source: U.S. Census Bureau, http://www.census.gov/eos/www/naics/

We tested the data we analyzed for internal consistency and for consistency with other key published studies, interviewed agency and industry officials regarding appropriate use of the data, and reviewed source data information regarding the entity's methodology and actions taken to ensure data reliability. We determined that the data were sufficiently reliable for our use. We note, however, that industry characteristics may change over time and may vary for firms within each sub-industry selected. To supplement our data analysis, we conducted interviews with industry groups such as steel, aluminum, chemicals, and the Energy-Intensive Manufacturer's Working Group.

Appendix 1

OBJECTIVES, SCOPE, AND METHODOLOGY

Objective 3

To identify and compare key features of proposed trade measures, we reviewed and analyzed selected climate change legislation introduced between 2007 and 2009, and congressional hearing records. From these documents we extracted information regarding features of the trade measures, such as objectives, scope of coverage, effective date for trade measures, and other key features. To identify how features of trade measures could address the potential economic and environmental effects of emissions pricing, we reviewed studies and reports obtained from our literature review, including past GAO reports on climate change and studies published by climate change policy institutes such as Resources for the Future, the Peterson Institute, and the Pew Center on Global Climate change. We also interviewed subject matter experts and agency officials from USTR; EPA; the Departments of Commerce, State, Energy, and Treasury, and CBP, regarding these issues and to identify the potential implementation and administrative challenges with using trade measures. In our interviews with agency officials we discussed steps agencies have taken to anticipate implementation challenges. To obtain information about climate change policies in other countries and to learn about the potential impact of U.S. trade measures on bilateral relations and international negotiations, we also interviewed officials from the embassies of Australia, Brazil, Canada, China, European Union, Mexico, and Singapore.

Objective 4

To assess potential international implications of using trade measures, we interviewed subject matter experts, agency officials in EPA, CBP, USTR, EIA, and the Departments of Treasury, State, and Commerce, and foreign embassy officials. To discuss questions and provisions that may be relevant in analyzing trade measures and output-based rebates for consistency with WTO rules, we reviewed WTO documents, obtained information from our interviews with subject-matter experts and agency officials, and reviewed information obtained from our literature review.

USTR provided technical comments on this report.

We conducted our work from October 2008 to July 2009 in accordance with all sections of GAO's Quality Assurance Framework that are relevant to our objectives. The framework requires that we plan and perform the engagement to obtain sufficient and appropriate evidence to meet our stated objectives and to discuss any limitations in our work. We believe that the information and data obtained, and the analysis conducted, provide a reasonable basis for any findings and conclusions in this product.

Appendix 2

NOTES TO INDUSTRY FIGURES

Notes to Figure 2: Energy intensity is calculated as the value of purchased fuels and electricity as a share of the value of output. Trade intensity is calculated as the value of total trade (exports plus imports) divided by the value of output plus imports. Data for value of output are from the Bureau of Economic Analysis Gross Domestic Product (GDP) by industry accounts, shipments by industry in current dollars.

Notes to Figure 3: Due to aggregation in source data, energy intensity for electrometallurgical products is assumed to be the same as iron and steel mills. Energy intensity data for primary aluminum is based on 2005 data. Aluminum products include industries characterized by the North American Industry Classification System (NAICS) with codes 331314 and 331316 and steel manufacturing industries represent codes 33121 and 33122.

Notes to Figure 4: Energy types characterized as "Renewables and other" includes residual and distillate fuel oil, liquefied petroleum gases, natural gas liquids, net steam (the sum of purchases, generation from renewables, and net transfers), and other energy that respondents indicated was used to produce heat and power or as feedstock/raw material inputs. Net electricity is the sum of purchases, transfers in, and generation from noncombustible renewable resources minus quantities sold and transferred out. Due to aggregation in source data, "Aluminum" includes primary aluminum and aluminum products.

Notes to Figure 5: "EU Plus" includes countries from the EU and other Annex I countries not represented elsewhere. Other than China, the largest two sources of imports for electrometallurgical products are the Republic of South Africa (17 percent) and Trinidad and Tobago (10 percent).

Notes to Figure 6: The current value of imports from all countries is shown in the table below the chart.

Notes to Figure 7: Energy intensity data for clay building materials are based on 2005 data because 2006 data were not available. Glass products include industries characterized by the North American Industry Classification System (NAICS) with codes 32721.

Notes to Figure 8: Energy use by type data for lime products excludes gypsum. Data on energy use by nonmetallic mineral sub-industry examples excluded from the chart are not currently reported by the Department of Energy.

Notes to Figure 9: After Canada and China, the two largest sources of imports for cement are Korea (9 percent) and Colombia (8 percent).

Notes to Figure 10: The current value of imports from all countries is shown in the table below the chart.

Appendix 2

NOTES TO INDUSTRY FIGURES

Notes to Figure 11: Due to aggregation in Bureau of Economic Analysis value of output data for paper mills with paperboard mills, value of output data for these two sub-industries are for 2006 and are from the Census Bureau's Annual Survey of Manufacturers, shipments by industry in current dollars. Aggregated data for 2006 are consistent between the two sources.

Notes to Figure 12: Data for coal and coke usage by pulp mills are not publicly available to avoid disclosure of individual firm information, such that percentage shares could not be computed. Data on energy use by paperboard containers is not currently reported by the Department of Energy.

Notes to Figure 14: The current value of imports from all countries is shown in the table below the chart.

Notes to Figure 15: Energy intensity data for alkalies and chlorine and carbon black is based on 2005 data because 2006 data is currently not available.

Notes to Figure 16: Data for certain energy uses by type for alkalies and chlorine, industrial gases, and artificial and synthetic fibers is not publicly available to avoid disclosure of individual firm information, such that percentage shares could not be computed.

Notes to Figure 17: Other than Canada, the two largest sources of imports for nitrogenous fertilizers are Trinidad and Tobago (26 percent) and the Middle East (14 percent), with countries in the Middle East defined by the U.S. Department of State.

Notes to Figure 18: The current value of imports from all countries is shown in the table below the chart.

Notes to Figure 19: In addition to these bills, Representatives John Dingell and Rick Boucher released a discussion draft on October 7, 2008. The discussion draft included a cap-and-trade proposal, and presents four options for allocating allowances under a cap-and-trade system.

Appendix 3

WORKS CITED

Aldy, Joseph E. and Pizer, William A. (May, 2009) "The Competitiveness Impacts of Climate Change Policies." Pew Center on Global Climate Change, Arlington, VA.

Fischer, Carolyn, and Fox, Alan K. (February, 2009) "Comparing Policies to Combat Emissions Leakage: Border Tax Adjustments versus Rebates." RFF Discussion Paper No. 09-02, Resources for the Future, Washington, D.C.

GAO, *Climate Change: Expert Opinion on the Economics of Policy Options to Address Climate Change*, GAO-08-605 (Washington, D.C.: May 9, 2008).

GAO, International Climate Change Programs: *Lessons Learned from the European Union's Emissions Trading Scheme and the Kyoto Protocol's Clean Development Mechanism*, GAO-09-151 (Washington, D.C.: November 18, 2008).

Ho, Mun S., Richard Morgenstern, and Jhih-Shyang Shih. (November, 2008) "Impact of Carbon Price Policies on U.S. Industry." RFF Discussion Paper No. 08-37, Resources for the Future, Washington, D.C.

U.S. Environmental Protection Agency, Office of Atmospheric Programs. EPA Preliminary Analysis of the Waxman-Markey Discussion Draft, The American Clean Energy and Security Act of 2009 in the 111th Congress, Apendix. April 20, 2009.

Appendix 4

CLIMATE CHANGE BILLS CITED IN REPORT

Save Our Climate Act of 2007, H.R. 2069, 110th Cong., (2007)

America's Energy Security Trust Fund Act of 2007, H.R. 3416, 110th Cong., (2007)

Low Carbon Economy Act of 2007, S. 1766, 110TH Cong., (2007)

Lieberman-Warner Climate Security Act of 2008, S. 3036, 110TH Cong., (2008)

Investing in Climate Action and Protection Act , H.R. 6186, 110TH Cong., (2008)

Climate Market, Auction, Trust & Trade Emissions Reduction System Act of 2008, H.R. 6316, 110TH Cong., (2008)

Carbon Leakage Prevention Act , H.R. 7146, 110TH Cong., (2008)

America's Energy Security Trust Fund Act of 2009, 111TH Cong., (2009)

Emission Migration Prevention with Long-term Output Yields Act , H.R. 1759, 111TH Cong., (2009)

American Clean Energy and Security Act of 2009 , H.R. 2454, 111TH Cong., (2009)

Appendix 5

GLOSSARY

- **Annex I Countries:** Parties to the United Nations Framework Convention on Climate Change (UNFCCC) that are industrialized countries and were members of the Organization for Economic Cooperation and Development (OECD) in 1992 plus countries characterized as economies in transition.

- **Allowances:** In the context of a cap-and-trade system, an emissions allowance is a permit to emit a specific quantity of emissions.

- **Border allowance requirement:** A measure that would require importers to purchase allowances from the federal government prior to importing goods into the United States.

- **Border tax adjustment:** A levy on imported goods proportionate to the imports' embedded carbon content. Generally, the levy on imported goods would be equivalent to the tax applied to domestic goods under a carbon tax system. Three legislative bills-- H.R. 2069, 110TH Cong. (2007), H.R. 3416, 110TH Cong. (2007), and H.R. 1337-- 111TH Cong. (2009), include provisions for a tax on any taxable carbon substance sold by the importer. For the purposes of this report, we are using the term border tax adjustment to refer to this tax described in the bills and to differentiate it from a carbon tax applied to domestic producers.

- **Business-as-usual:** A scenario in which no action is taken to reduce greenhouse gas emissions.

- **Cap-and-trade:** An emissions pricing system in which the government applies an aggregate cap or quota to limit total emissions from regulated sources, which are required to hold allowances to cover their emissions. Allowances are allocated by the government and may be traded. Sources whose allowances exceed their emissions may offer permits for sale, while sources for which emissions exceed allowances will need to buy them.

- **Carbon dioxide equivalent:** The quantity of carbon dioxide emissions that would trap as much heat as a quantity of non-carbon-dioxide gases, such as methane, sulfur hexafluoride, nitrous oxide, or industrial gases.

- **Carbon leakage:** The condition when emissions reductions in one country are replaced by increases in emissions in other countries.

- **Carbon offsets:** Reductions in greenhouse gas emissions from an activity in one place to compensate for emissions released elsewhere.

- **Carbon tax system:** A system that requires regulated sources to pay a charge based on the level of their emissions.

Appendix 5

GLOSSARY

- **Competitiveness:** The ability of a U.S. industry to compete successfully in international markets with foreign competitors.

- **Cost containment measures**: Mechanisms designed to reduce the economic impact of climate change legislation on certain regulated entities and provide them with flexibility in managing compliance costs. Examples include banking and borrowing of allowances, price caps on allowances, free allocation of allowances, and carbon offsets.

- **Dispute Settlement Body**: The WTO's dispute settlement process is administered by the Dispute Settlement Body, composed of representatives from WTO Members, and rules set time limits for each step in the process. .

- **Downstream regulation**: Regulation on sources that emit greenhouse gases.

- **Embedded carbon content**: Carbon emissions associated with the production of a product through the entirety of its supply chain.

- **Emissions pricing**: A market-based mechanism, such as a carbon tax or cap-and-trade system, to encourage reductions in emissions by putting a price on them. In this report, "emissions pricing" refers to greenhouse gas emissions pricing, as opposed to pricing systems for other types of emissions.

- **Energy intensity:** The industry's cost of purchased electricity and fuel costs, or energy expenditures, divided by the value of shipments (output) of the industry, as defined in H.R. 2454.

- **Free allowance allocation:** Emission allowances given by the government for free. Under a cap-and-trade program governments can either give allowances to regulated entities for free or they can sell allowances through an auction. Allocating allowances for free represents a transfer of wealth from the government to the entities receiving the allowances, while auctioning allowances enables the government to decide how to use the revenue.

- **Greenhouse gas intensity:** Twenty times the quantity of carbon dioxide equivalent emissions from a sector, divided by the value of shipments (output) for the sector, as defined in H.R. 2454.

- **Greenhouse gases:** Gases such as carbon dioxide, methane, nitrous oxide, and other substances that increase temperatures by trapping heat that would otherwise escape the earth's atmosphere.

- **Intergovernmental Panel on Climate Change (IPCC):** A scientific intergovernmental body set up by the World Meteorological Organization (WMO) and by the United Nations Environment Program (UNEP). The IPCC was established to provide decision makers and others interested in climate change with an objective source of information about climate change.

Appendix 5

GLOSSARY

- **International reserve allowance:** Under a cap-and-trade system, the United States could require importers to acquire emissions allowances corresponding to the level of greenhouse gases emitted during production.

- **Output-based rebates:** Rebates based on actual, recent measures of production that are given to regulated sources in a cap-and-trade system for allowances they have purchased to cover their emissions.

- **Trade intensity:** The ratio of the sum of the value of imports and exports within an industry to the sum of the value of shipments (output) and imports within an industry, as defined in H.R. 2454.

- **Trade measures:** Cost equalization measures at the border that impose a cost or other requirement on energy-intensive imports from countries with weaker climate policies. Depending on the type of domestic carbon mitigation system in place, trade measures can take several forms. For example, trade measures can be proposed as part of a cap-and-trade system (allowance requirement at the border) or a carbon tax system (border tax).

- **Upstream regulation:** Greenhouse gas regulation focused on the sale of fuels that produce greenhouse gases when they are used.

- **WTO Appellate Body:** A body within the WTO's that reviews a WTO panel's legal findings during a dispute resolution process. The Appellate Body and the Appellate Body's report is to be accepted by parties in the dispute unless the Dispute Settlement Body decides by consensus not to adopt the report.

GAO's Mission	The Government Accountability Office, the audit, evaluation, and investigative arm of Congress, exists to support Congress in meeting its constitutional responsibilities and to help improve the performance and accountability of the federal government for the American people. GAO examines the use of public funds; evaluates federal programs and policies; and provides analyses, recommendations, and other assistance to help Congress make informed oversight, policy, and funding decisions. GAO's commitment to good government is reflected in its core values of accountability, integrity, and reliability.
Obtaining Copies of GAO Reports and Testimony	The fastest and easiest way to obtain copies of GAO documents at no cost is through GAO's Web site (www.gao.gov). Each weekday afternoon, GAO posts on its Web site newly released reports, testimony, and correspondence. To have GAO e-mail you a list of newly posted products, go to www.gao.gov and select "E-mail Updates."
Order by Phone	The price of each GAO publication reflects GAO's actual cost of production and distribution and depends on the number of pages in the publication and whether the publication is printed in color or black and white. Pricing and ordering information is posted on GAO's Web site, http://www.gao.gov/ordering.htm. Place orders by calling (202) 512-6000, toll free (866) 801-7077, or TDD (202) 512-2537. Orders may be paid for using American Express, Discover Card, MasterCard, Visa, check, or money order. Call for additional information.
To Report Fraud, Waste, and Abuse in Federal Programs	Contact: Web site: www.gao.gov/fraudnet/fraudnet.htm E-mail: fraudnet@gao.gov Automated answering system: (800) 424-5454 or (202) 512-7470
Congressional Relations	Ralph Dawn, Managing Director, dawnr@gao.gov, (202) 512-4400 U.S. Government Accountability Office, 441 G Street NW, Room 7125 Washington, DC 20548
Public Affairs	Chuck Young, Managing Director, youngc1@gao.gov, (202) 512-4800 U.S. Government Accountability Office, 441 G Street NW, Room 7149 Washington, DC 20548

www.ingramcontent.com/pod-product-compliance
Lightning Source LLC
Chambersburg PA
CBHW080341290526

45791CB00009BA/2680